Dare to Follow

Suzanne Pillans

New Life Press

New Life Press
PO Box 17
Chichester
England PO20 6YB

New Life Press is an imprint of New Wine Ministries

ISBN: 1 903725 10 0

Other books available by the same author:

Search for Truth – a book of prose and poetry revealing God through the beauty of nature.

The Biblical Approach to Basic Horsemanship – a book giving the basics and attitudes to handling and riding horses, or handling any animal, as the Bible shows us to.

Typeset by CRB Associates, Reepham, Norfolk.
Printed in England by Clays Ltd, St Ives plc.

Contents

Preface

Suzanne was born in Bournemouth and grew up with horses. She became a Christian through the miraculous healing of her horse, Jacky Boy, and then dedicated her life to the Lord.

She is now married to Wilfrid. They have a daughter named Rebecca, and they went to Bible College together.

Suzanne and Wilfred have dared to follow God as the Bible says, and through doing so, the Lord has led them into an exciting life of faith and ministry. Hence the title of this book – *Dare to Follow*.

Foreword

In the short time that I have known Suzanne and Wilfrid Pillans, I have been very impressed with their radical faith, passion for Jesus and determination to pursue God's call upon their lives.

When I was first shown around their riding school in Oxfordshire, I was thrilled to learn of how God had supernaturally intervened to enable them to build the place. One testimony after another of God's provision and strength revealed the unique anointing they carry.

This book, which is the story of Suzanne's journey with God, reveals something of God's faithfulness to those who are willing to follow Him wholeheartedly.

I believe this book will challenge you and inspire you to go further with God than you have ever gone. I hope it leads you into an adventure of faith for yourself.

Clive Corfield
Lancaster
(Director of Sovereign Ministries)

Chapter 1

The Background

I am something else – something feminine and emotional – or something struggling within an iron grip, a grip of control – a girl who wants to escape – to fly with the music of the wind – to laugh with the movement of life – to... I shook awake. The bus was skidding into a screeching halt with a flat tyre.

We all leapt from the bus and a man bustled around finding the tools to fit the new wheel. It was still dark, almost 5.00 am, and a cock in the distance shrilled the air that dawn was soon to break.

I stayed alone, away from the chattering men and women who were on their way to visit their children at boarding school. Who was I anyway? Just one unhappy girl, and as time came for us to re-board the bus, I seated myself again in my chosen corner, again to be caught up in my thoughts.

It was a long story; it started a few years back, eight to be exact. I was 14 years old; my parents had given me my greatest desire, a pony of my own. Blity was his name and though not the easiest of ponies, I loved him.

I had not owned Blity for more than six months when the tragedy happened. Playing in the lunging ring he had reared up, lost his balance and come down on his back, breaking it on impact. It was a terrible thing for me, and it seemed to me that all nice things just came to an end.

It was a month later that we moved to a beautiful farm in Banhoek. Fruit orchards and grape vines nestled in the valleys, while the majestic mountains of the Cape ruggedly sheltered them with pine trees, and waterfalls fell into large rivers giving plentiful water for irrigation. This was the beginning of my long search for the truth.

It was during that time that I came in contact with Jacky Boy, then a naughty one-month-old foal. His mother was a Perseron mare called Bess. She pulled the plough between the vines until one day, a racehorse stallion from the next door stud jumped the fence and Bess was in foal.

Jacky grew quickly and soon became a nuisance on the farm. He would drink the cow's milk, jump the grape vines and even got into the vegetable patch. It was then that Jeremy, the owner of the farm, approached Joy to take Jacky Boy over.

I was delighted and later Joy gave him to me.

The next day Jacky was transported to us. I spent every spare moment I had with him. He was quite a character and daily we worked together on long reins, until he became so obedient to the voice that he was a joy. We became so close to each other that when I got sick with jaundice, he spent the full three weeks outside my window until I was well again. One day when I was washing my hair, but still not allowed to go outside, Jacky put his head through the bathroom window, took hold of the big plastic bottle of family shampoo, and after squirting it over the bathroom, suddenly took off with it. The next moment I was chasing after Jacky with a towel around my head. It got me outside again anyway.

During the next two years Jacky Boy grew into a fine looking horse standing 16.3 hands high.

By this time I had left school and was enjoying the freedom of being at home, when suddenly my father was transferred to Port Elizabeth. As a result, we had to uproot ourselves and moved to the port town some 800 miles away.

This meant getting Jacky gelded as he would have to be stabled out, and it was with reluctance that we left the beautiful Cape.

Port Elizabeth opened a new chapter for me and I soon got my first job as a riding instructor. It had been my goal in life to own my own riding school and while my teaching was proving to be a success, I became more and more ambitious, until one day six months later I gave in my notice and ventured out on my own, under my parents' watchful eyes.

We only had five acres of land and within six months we had ten horses and sixty pupils, so my parents decided to move to bigger premises.

We rented a large property on the Kragga Kamma Road and during the next four years Kragga Kamma Riding School flourished, growing into an establishment of sixty-four horses and around a hundred pupils a week, but still something was missing.

I was not qualified: I must be qualified – that's the answer. So leaving my parents to take over the Riding School and employ another instructor, I set off for England.

After six months' training at Wirral Riding and Saddlery Centre, I sat my Horsemanship exams. I then spent some time in Europe going from country to country studying the different approaches to horsemanship and gaining valuable experience.

At 22 years old I returned to South Africa and now, too proud to return to Port Elizabeth, preferred rather to test my standards with the top riding schools of the country.

It was a month later that I signed a lease at a riding centre in Honeydew. Jacky Boy, who had been well cared for while I was overseas, joined me and soon we were hard at work building up our second riding school. Kildare had been closed down for two years, so it was necessary to begin again from scratch.

Things went well for us and Kildare was making a profit within three months. Again I had around a hundred pupils a week and, though successful, I just seemed to grow weary. Still something was missing.

Maybe I haven't done well enough in the show ring – that's the answer. So back to work schooling up my horses, Jacky as well. Every weekend we were at horse shows. Here again my horses did well. Jacky was a good high jumping horse, seldom touching a jump, but he was not fast enough in speed events. Gunflash was doing well as a C grade and jumped superbly at the Epol Indoor Show, but the best jumper I had was a 14.2 hand pony called Ginger Square. Being extremely athletic and bold, he surprised everybody by taking me up to B grade. Again we were on the way to becoming successful, but still something was missing. It seemed that at every achievement the bubble just popped. Inside, I really had nothing. Could trophies really fill that gap? It seemed to me that I'd rather lose something, as with every cup I won came either opposition or the loss of someone who I thought was a friend.

Where am I going? I thought. Where is the answer? There must be something more, something beyond competitions and jealousies, striving and achieving – achieving for what? But at least I had Jacky Boy; at least he was a true friend.

It was two weeks later when it happened; now only five weeks ago. I bit my lip and looked out of the bus window. It was now light and the sun began to cast long rays of light over the green hills of Natal, lighting up the round thatch-roofed clay dwellings of the Zulu Tribe.

Only five weeks ago and so much had happened. I had been riding Gunflash home from a nearby horse show and leading Jacky Boy. One of my pupils, a young man, was riding Ginger.

We had almost arrived at the stables, when suddenly a car came speeding towards us on the wrong side of the road. 'Get out of the way,' I screamed to Mike, and got my horses as close to the wire fence as possible. But it was already too late. With a deathly thud the car had hit us and Jacky's reins were torn from my hand.

I was stunned and yet still astride Gunflash. I did not want to turn round, but had to. To my horror Ginger was dead, his rider thrown to the ground, and Jacky with his leg ripped to an odd angle was breathing heavily. 'Mike, are you OK?' I screamed, dismounting from my horse.

'Fine, fine,' he replied, 'but I can't move my leg. Call the ambulance.'

By this time I was at Jacky's side and seeing he was still alive, gave him a quick pat, leapt on Gunflash and galloped full speed to the stables, then throwing Gunflash's reins into the hands of an alarmed student, rushed for the phone.

Soon the ambulance arrived and a horsebox was on its way. Ginger, who had taken the worst of the hit, saving his rider's life, was dragged to the side of the road. Mike, who had been thrown over the car roof, was now sitting up. He was lifted onto a stretcher and wheeled into the ambulance. His leg, we discovered later, was broken in three places, which meant three months in hospital.

As the ambulance drove off, I left Jacky still lying down and rushed to the corner of the road where I was to meet the horsebox.

Ten minutes later we were back and to my joy Jacky was now standing up, but with one leg apparently useless.

We struggled to get him aboard the horsebox with only three legs, and after a nightmare journey of trying to keep him balanced, we arrived at the vet and again struggled off the box and into a stable.

The damage was serious and the vet worked on him all night. He removed the glass at arm's length under Jacky's shoulder and stitched up the foot-long tear from the crest of his neck down to the shoulder, but the damage was more serious. His shoulder was broken in two places, at the scapula and humerus, leaving the shoulder joint loose under the skin. One could even move it with one's hand.

Three days later the horse was sent to Onderstepoort, the best-equipped horse hospital in South Africa, but they refused to pin the bones together as even more damage had been done. The nerve of the deltoid muscle had been severed right through and without this muscle, which is the largest muscle of the shoulder, there would be nothing to keep the shoulder in place, even if the bones could knit together. In a horse the front legs are not connected to the skeleton of the horse, but instead are held in place by powerful muscles.

I insisted they kept on trying to save Jacky, so they began to massage the muscles daily, hoping that the nerve would recover.

Meanwhile, I had to carry on at Kildare Riding Centre and, on top of the normal lessons, I had to arrange for the coming of the 'Singing Horsemen' from the Drakersberg Boy Choir School in Natal. They were to give one of their performances in our floodlit arena.

The following Saturday they arrived and put on a good show. After the people had left, I helped them with their horses and got to know a couple of the boys, Dion and Gavin, then in standard six. It was then that their instructor approached me and, not realizing that I ran Kildare, offered me a job, not a well paid job, but with free board and lodgings. I said I would think about it.

I did think about it. On one hand, where was I really going? What was I really achieving at Kildare? I lived alone in a small flat, extremely busy in the day and too tired for anything at night. I was maybe earning 500 Rand per month, a good wage for a single girl. But then what was the use of money, when you had everything you needed already – except, of course, in a case like Jacky Boy's?

Maybe it would be a good idea to accept this job after all. If I could not find what I was looking for in Johannesburg, maybe I would find it in Natal. People could not help me, culture and society could not help me, history could not help me, success could not help me. In fact, I felt totally lost in my search, for I could not even define for myself what I was actually looking for. I had searched hard for it, not only in South Africa, but also in England, and eleven countries of Europe, but I could not find the answer. Something was still missing.

So even though against my own logic of giving up 500 Rand per month, for 100 Rand per month, I decided to take the chance and at least see the place. So I joined the parents on the 300-mile trip to the Drakensberg for parents' weekend.

Chapter 2

Parents' Weekend

By now we were approaching the foothills of the berg. We left the tar road and began a gradual ascent on the muddy farm roads. We could not see the mountains for they were hidden by cloud and as we came nearer, we left the sun-drenched valley for the shadows of the clouded berg.

They must have had a lot of rain and in some places we were skidding so much that we had to slow down to some 5 kilometres an hour.

Now we were passing beautiful pine forests and the cold, sweet mountain air began to circulate round the bus.

'We will soon be there,' someone exclaimed, and the parents started chatting about their children.

The last stretch was the worst. A very steep hairpin bend was approaching and the bus began to skid sideways. Though it was in first gear, it just didn't seem to make any progress. Some of us, seeing the 100 foot drop, preferred to get out, and noticing some of the boys running to meet us, decided it was a good idea. So we jumped off the bus and left it to its 2 kilometre per hour progress.

Gavin was amongst the boys who came to meet us. 'So you did come?' he said. 'I thought you might change your mind.'

'Why should I do that?' I replied.

'Race you to the trees,' he shouted.

The boys were off and then waited for us to catch up at a walking pace. They wanted to beat the bus home, but their parents were not that keen, as progress on the steep road was hard enough, even at the slower pace.

To the left green valleys rose to the foothills of the mountains ahead of us, while to the right we passed the home of Mr Pearce, the author of *Barrier of Spears*, and another home of a retired couple, before turning into the farm.

Rusted split-pole fences showed the way into the large double-story home, with white fluffy bantams scurrying into the kitchen yard. The boys took us through the kitchen, where two Zulu ladies were stirring something in a large pot on an old-fashioned coal stove. We then removed our boots and walked into the lounge.

John was there to meet us. 'Welcome, welcome,' he said. 'Do sit down. How was the trip? Where are the others?'

'Coming,' Mrs Gay replied. 'The bus had difficulty with the muddy road, so we walked.'

'Good for you,' replied John.

'Lina,' he shouted, 'bring some tea.'

'By the way,' he said turning to us, 'anyone want coffee?'

'And three coffees Lina, please.'

John was a broad man of middle height, with thick black eyebrows matching his thick black hair. He was around forty years of age, very outgoing and friendly, and known for his musical talents. Artistic, and brilliant at his profession. He was also the founder of the Drakensberg Boys Choir School.

'We've a good programme for the weekend,' he went on. 'Lunch at one, then we will go down to the school. At 2.30 pm we will be having sports – a couple of races for the parents as well, supper at 6.00 pm and then the boys are putting on a play and a few songs.'

'Tomorrow, church at 9.00 am in the chapel. We have a priest coming in from Winterton to lead the service and after that we have organised a braai and the bus will leave for Johannesburg at 2.30 pm.'

'Ah! I believe that's the bus at last.'

We all got up.

'I was just going to call the tractor to give you a tug,' said John, greeting them.

'Just got a bit stuck above S-bend,' replied the driver. 'Had to collect some rocks to help drive out of it.'

'Anyway, come in and have some nice hot tea or coffee,' said John, turning round, 'and then I'll show you your rooms and you can get your cases in. Quite safe on the bus, don't worry,' he then said to one of the parents.

We all trudged back into the lounge, when Dion came up and said, 'Oh Sue. We're so glad you came. Come, let us show you the horses.'

'All right,' I replied.

We were soon walking down to the slanting buildings and along a passage where six Arab horses were busy munching hay.

'This is Sharida,' said Dion, pointing at a chestnut with a blaze down her face. 'And this is Sharon,' also a chestnut with a blaze, but slightly smaller. 'And this is Shah,' a small grey gelding about 14.2 hands high and a bit common looking. 'We bought this one recently,' said Dion, 'but she has got some Arab blood.' Dion then went on to introduce me to Falcon, a beautiful grey Arab with a classical head and neck with a long lush main and good conformation, Poppet a small chestnut pony mare, also with a blaze and a part-Arab bay gelding.

'Now to show you our champion.' Dion went round to a closed stable. 'This is Silver Leaf, our stallion.'

An elegant grey head appeared over the door with his ears pricked. Yes he was a fine horse and his coat was shinning silver in the patches of sunlight that were coming through the clouds now and then.

'And over there in the field is Fatty Boom Cracker,' Dion went on. 'Of course that's not her real name, but you should ride her. It's like sitting on a balloon.' She too was a bay. 'That's all of them,' said Dion.

He then showed me the tack room equipped with sheepskin saddles, a couple of English leather saddles and eight snaffle bridles, two double bridles and one lunge. Each boy had his own grooming kit, which was numbered and kept on small shelves.

At this moment Gavin came rushing in. 'Is Suzanne here?' he asked. 'John is looking for her.'

I then said thanks to Dion for showing me around and went along with Gavin.

The meeting with John went well. We went over what was required from the boys, how we fitted in with the boys choir school and the different teams. There were only eight boys on the national team and 52 boys for general riding lessons each week. The national team were to be trained daily and I would have to choose a completely new team apart from Dion, Gavin and a boy called Taubin. The rest of the team were going into standard 8, so of course had to leave for High School.

'Will you be able to get them up to standard in 3 months?' asked John. 'That's with two lessons a day, for our first tour in May.'

'I hope so,' I replied. 'Can they all ride at present?'

'Not well,' said John, 'but I'm sure you can do it. Anyway,' he continued, 'I want your decision by tomorrow.'

I left his office thoughtfully. Quite a tall order to have to fully set up a show with five beginners out of eight riders by May. *The History of the Horse* included scenes out of Arabian culture, Roman culture, long reining, lunging, a musical ride, a duet and a comedy. I had never done anything like this in my life. Could I even do it? My only experience of this sort of thing was my pleasant year under the Major with his Lipizzaner Team. There we would put on a show every Sunday morning, but his horses had had years of training and we were all accomplished riders. To do a similar thing with beginners, and children at that, seemed to be almost impossible. Anyway it would certainly be a challenge, if nothing else.

The afternoon went quickly and soon the sound of exciting races died down and we had supper, saw the boys sing, drove back up to John's house and went to bed.

The next morning dawned with thick mountain mist. It had rained during the night and I was hoping to at least see the mountains before we returned to Johannesburg, but it appeared that the mist just wasn't going to lift.

I got up and went down with the other parents for a good breakfast of eggs, bacon, tomatoes, onions and fet cooks. After that we got into the Land Rovers and drove down to the school for the church service.

The clouds still hung low, the mists having lifted only to the treetops. A couple of Springbok deer stepped gingerly through large puddles in the park, then lifted their heads and were gone.

The schoolboys were now seated in the chapel and some of their parents had joined them. I stepped in with the last few and seated myself close to the window.

The elderly priest stood and the organ stopped playing. 'Good morning,' he announced.

'Hello,' replied a small girl.

At that the people turned, a few suppressed laughs escaping, causing a grin to spread over the face of the white-headed priest. At that the boys, taking advantage, allowed their giggles to escape, and it took a few minutes until all was quiet.

We said a prayer and then the boys' choir filed in and lined up in their places. They were dressed in red jackets, which somehow showed the innocent looking faces of the twenty-four singing horsemen that were to sing that day.

The audience rose and sang, 'Fill the world with love'. It was then that I turned towards the window and saw the beauty revealing itself in the most spectacular way. The mist had ascended and the sun shone its way through the lifting clouds, which gradually unveiled the most magnificent picture of soaring peaks. Down below a buck had returned and an ostrich was stretching his wings.

It was beautiful service and as we walked out, I asked the little girl who had said 'Hello' whether she had been good.

'Oh yes,' she replied. 'A man came and offered me a plate of money and I said "no thank you."'

The boys then came up, all talking at once. 'Are you coming to teach us next year? When are you coming? Can I show you the zebras?'

'I would love to see the zebras,' I replied. So we walked along the outside of their camp until we could see them. There was a young foal there as well.

'Only two weeks old,' one of the boys explained, 'but we're not allowed to go in.'

'Why?' I asked.

'Because of Henry.'

'Who's he?' I asked.

'The ostrich. You see, he used to be free in the park but there was this little old lady who came to the shop to buy some bread. Henry wanted some, so he followed her. But the lady was scared of him and walked faster, so Henry walked faster. Then the lady began to jog and Henry began to go faster too. Then,' he went on, 'she was really scared and ran for her life, dropping the basket as she went. Henry then went and ate the bread, but the poor lady, she nearly had a coronary and died. After that Henry began to chase everybody, so he has to be locked up in the game park for good now.'

'Anyway, he's a thief,' another boy went on. 'My mother came to the park with her caravan to give me my birthday party and when we were not looking that Henry stretched his neck into our tent and ate up all the cakes.'

'Come and see my porcupine,' yet another boy insisted. 'We keep him in the school kitchen yard.'

'But ain't they dangerous?'

'Oh no,' he replied, 'not this one.'

So we all went up to the school, and as we went in we were met by a dog and a three-legged lamb coming down the staircase.

'What's this?' I exclaimed.

'Oh her?' said a small boy. 'We rescued her and brought her up on the bottle. She's part of the school now.'

The time just flew by. All those lovely animals. The porcupine was asleep so we didn't disturb him. What a school! It was more like a child's dream school and I just fell in love with it, and all the boys.

'Yes,' I decided. I would accept the job.

Jacky Boy (1 day before the healing) – bones still broken after 6 weeks

Jacky Boy (after the healing) – a white patch on his hind quarters due to pigmentation loss is the only reminder of when he kept falling down

Chapter 3

Jacky Boy

The journey back to Johannesburg went smoothly, though now my thoughts had returned to Jacky Boy. 'What if the massaging is not working? But surely it is working,' I tried to reassure myself. 'Anyway first thing tomorrow, I'm going to visit him.'

We arrived late that night, so I said goodbye to the parents and Mrs Gay, who had been sitting next to me in the bus, had a look at the horses and went to bed.

Next morning I was up early in the stables, which Patrick, my manager, had been caring for while I was away. I had to get out to Onderstepoort to see Jacky, so as soon as morning stables was over, I was on my way.

It was a good hour's drive to Onderstepoort and the grass was still yellow and dry in Johannesburg after the winter. The summer rains had not come to the Johannesburg region as yet. I put my foot on the accelerator, going as fast as the speed limit would allow, then had to slow down again and work my way through Pretoria. I had slight difficulty finding the Onderstepoort road but once I found it, it was only a further ten-minute ride.

I turned in the long driveway, drove up to the stables and made my way to the office. Soon they found the vet who was in charge of my horse and we made our way to Jacky's stable.

'I'm afraid the massage has not worked,' he told me. 'The nerve was apparently severed right through and once that has happened, there is no hope of restoring the muscle,' he explained. 'I'm afraid that you are going to have to put the horse down, for without the muscle, it is impossible to pin the bones together,' he went on.

I stared down at the wet newly-washed red-brick passage and the smell of Jays fluid stung my nostrils, along with the worst news I felt I had ever heard. 'I can't do it. I just can't do it.'

We turned into a large dark barn with large well kept stables down each side, complete with large red and black sliding doors, and walked about half-way down the central passage.

The vet said, 'here's your horse on the right.'

I could not believe my eyes when I saw Jacky. He was so thin, so miserable, and he hardly even seemed to recognize me. All I could do was grab hold of his neck and cry into his mane.

'We had to get him a bit thinner,' the vet explained. 'We had to get as much weight as possible off his bad leg, if we wanted to have any chance of getting him right.'

I remained silent. The only thing I could think of was getting Jacky back to the stables as soon as possible. Then I would think about the next step. I realized that the vets really had done all they could do for him. I thanked them for this and after telling them of my plans to collect Jacky within the next few days, left for home.

As soon as I got home I made some phone calls and managed to arrange with Bill to collect Jacky with his horse box the following Friday. The next three days dragged terribly though, for I had to face the terrible decision of whether to have Jacky put down. At least the busy riding school was able to keep my mind occupied, and it was only after work that it was especially difficult.

Soon Friday arrived. I drove over to Bill's stables and we were on our way to collect Jacky.

When we arrived, Jacky was looking just as dejected as on Monday. I placed his halter over his nose, did it up and attempted to lead him out of his stable. This was not so easy, as he could not use his fore leg at all, and had to hobble on his near fore and hind legs. After quite some time and with much effort and struggle we got him at last out into the sunlight and loaded him into the truck. We then had to place a wide strap under him and secure him to the truck, so that with the extra support he would not fall down on the journey home. I then rushed back into the horse hospital for his progress charts which showed his deteriation while he was there, said goodbye to the vet and got back into the truck.

They drove the truck back as slowly and gently as possible, while I held onto Jacky and fed him handfuls of lucerne; at least his appetite had not been affected.

Instead of taking Jacky Boy back to Kildare Riding Centre where there was no grazing, and where the children would be utterly upset when they saw him, I decided to take him to a friend's farm nearby. Here Jacky Boy would be quiet and have plenty of grazing. I could visit him alone every day and treat him with plenty of carrots and affection during the last few days of his life.

I now disregarded all the vet's instructions to keep him in a dark stable, for there was nothing further man could do for him anyway. So why not let him be out in the sunlight?

We soon arrived and I unloaded him with as much difficulty as loading him, and led him hobbling into his small paddock with plenty of grass. I then tightened the harness that I made, to keep his shoulder bones as close to his body as possible, and after a feed returned home.

At least Jacky Boy was in no pain. That was something, but his disability must have been quite some burden to him. I then realized that I had to do it. I had to phone the vet to put him down.

I dialled the number feeling like I was about to ask for my closest friend to be shot. It was horrid.

'Can I help you?' asked the vet on the other end.

'Yes.' I replied. 'It's about Jacky Boy, about having him put down.'

'You've made the right decision,' he said. 'It's cruel, you know, to keep a horse in that condition alive. I'm so glad that you have been able to make this decision.'

'Thank you,' I replied, 'but could you give him just a few more days before putting him down? He's not in pain and I do want him to feel just a little happier. He still loves his food and I've bought him some carrots. I just want to spoil him a little first.'

'How about next Thursday then?' asked the vet.

'That's fine,' I said.

'Right, see you then. Goodbye.'

'Goodbye.'

I replaced the receiver. The vet had been so nice to me and I knew that theoretically it was the right decision, yet still something within me was not giving up. Surely somehow there was still hope.

The afternoon went slowly. Two riding lessons to give and just after the 3.00 pm lesson the clouds opened up and it poured. We all rode for cover and we had to wait a good half-hour until we could start the next class. Now we would have to rearrange the classes for the summer months again. It is amazing, but in Johannesburg it nearly always rains at the same time every day in summer and lasts about the same length of time, so by moving the 4.00 pm class later, one could normally carry on teaching almost unhindered by the rain.

Then I had to tell the pupils about my coming move to Natal and that Patrick would be taking over Kildare from me, and would be teaching them in the future. Most of the pupils knew Patrick already, so apart from some of the children who did not want me to go, it seemed that the transition would go smoothly.

Saturday was especially busy and on Sunday we had a horse show to go to, so it was quite hectic. Even though I was not riding myself, I had ponies to plait up and pupils to prepare for the classes and then jumping courses to walk with them. They did quite well and won a couple of tickets in the jumping events and one in a showing class. Apart from this, I had to fit in seeing Jacky Boy twice a day and had problems with him falling down. Once he fell down he could not get up again, so we had to help him up with three poles, a band under his girth and a pulley. This worked quite well but I realised that this could not go on either.

That Sunday night when the last of the pupils had gone, I felt particularly miserable and lonely. It had been particularly hard having lost Ginger in the car accident and we had certainly missed him at the horse show today. Now Jacky too, my best friend and most loved horse, was about to be put down as well.

'Why must he suffer? What has he done wrong? Or maybe what have I done wrong? What is the reason for this? What must I do now? What have I done so far? Cry and mope over him? Jacky means so much to me, does He want me to suffer over him? What can I do for him? There is nothing I can do.'

Do I carry on moping and crying over him until I am sick too? I'm still all right, and I must not give up. I must carry on.

How? Stop being depressed. How? Look at the best side of things. Everything happens for a reason. Why? No one knows. Is it punishment that in some way we deserve? Maybe to test us, to harden us up for something. We must be strong enough to accept anything. If we are not, we fail, and I am failing now. I must accept this thing. I must go ahead and make the best of things, to try and do my best. Jesus died for us, didn't He? Maybe I must prove that I can accept this for Him. Maybe we are on earth to do a job and to prove ourselves worthy. Maybe we are also here to be prepared for something unknown. Should not being an honest and worthy person come first in one's life?

What were these thoughts coming through my mind? I suddenly realised they were Christian thoughts. I had not been to church for ages apart from parents weekend. In fact, the last time was in England, and that was just for the adventure of following the sound of bells through the woods. I ended up in the quaintest little village at a most beautiful moss-covered church. It was as if the bells had called me there, and I decided that I may as well go in. Though it had been quite a beautiful service, it had nothing to offer me. It was nice to listen to the singing and a few pleasant sounding words from the minister, but that was all.

Now I was, in my desperation over Jacky Boy, thinking Christian thoughts. Maybe there is some truth in all this. Maybe God did create the heavens and the earth and everything in it; after all I was brought up to believe so and yet somehow it had not meant that much.

Yet if God did create the universe and every human being and animal that walked this earth, then He would also have the power to re-create them.

That's it, that's the one thing I have not tried for Jacky Boy. I have not prayed for him. But how can I come to God and pray for a horse, when I haven't even gone to church? I thought, why should He help me, when I've done nothing for Him?

'Please Lord, help me,' I cried. 'Forgive me please. Lord, I want to believe in You, and I know that if You are alive today that You have the power to hear this prayer and that You also have the power to heal my horse. Please Lord, if You can hear me, forgive me for my unbelief.'

'Lord, if You are really hearing me, please forgive me for not coming to You in prayer before and for asking You to help me now. Please Lord, if it is Your will please heal my horse, just enough that he can move around more easily without pain and I will care for him, realizing he will never be fully sound. Then, Lord, I will know You are truly real, and I will then serve You for the rest of my life.'

'Please, Lord, give me the strength from this moment on to forget my own unhappiness, to wake up out of my depression, to try hard and go ahead with my work for You. I must be strong and set an example. Please, Lord, help me to find my security in You, rather than in a horse. Please, Lord, be my friend and I will try, from now on.'

The next morning I woke with a new expectancy. 'Had God heard my prayer,' echoed through my mind, 'or am I going mad?' I did not dare tell anyone about last night. They for sure would think I was mad. I just had to get out to Jacky and the sooner the better.

I rushed through the morning stables and was soon on my way to see him. I just seemed to get more and more excited and yet I could not figure out why. Didn't I ask God to do the impossible last night? Still I would not believe those thoughts, I just got more and more excited. As yet, I had no right to believe that God should help me, yet something within me would not give up.

At last I was there. I leaped out of the car and ran towards the paddock. On reaching it, I opened the gate and called Jacky Boy.

Jacky Boy hobbled up. He looked just the same. I turned round and walked away. Jacky Boy followed me. Disappointment began to sting my eyes. 'But what can I expect? Am I expecting a miracle or something? I don't know, I just don't know.' I felt so mixed up; maybe I had to give up Jacky for Jesus. Had I not prayed last night that I should find my security in God rather than in a horse? That meant that if God healed Jacky, then Jacky must no longer be the most important thing to me, he must not be quite so close as a friend, God must come first in all those things in my life and this is what I was prepared to do.

What if God was not going to heal Jacky? Would I be able to give him up for God, like Jesus gave up His life for us? I had made the phone call, the vet was coming. I thought and hoped that my answer would be yes.

'Your horse has fallen down,' screeched in my ears.

I turned round. Jacky Boy had fallen and my friend who shouted to me was running towards us from the house.

Suddenly Jacky Boy heaved his hindquarters up like a cow with his hind legs, powerfully lifted himself up onto all four legs, turned round and to our gaping mouths trotted using all four legs. I couldn't believe my eyes.

'The Lord's healed my horse,' I shouted. 'He has really healed my horse.'

Utta looked at me in astonishment.

'I'll tell you later,' I told her, crying for joy. 'Please, Utta, may I use your phone?'

'Sure,' she said. 'What for?'

'To tell the vet not to come,' I shouted, running towards the house.

I hastily picked up the receiver and dialled the number. 'Is the vet there?' I inquired.

'Yes, hold on, I'll put you through.'

'Hello, hello.'

'Oh, hello doctor, I've got some fantastic news for you. Oh, it's Suzanne here. The Lord has just healed Jacky Boy.'

'Repeat that please,' asked the vet.

'The Lord has just healed Jacky Boy,' I repeated.

'Are you sure you're OK?' the vet asked.

'Of course I am. I just wanted to tell you that the Lord has healed Jacky, so you won't need to come and put him down on Thursday.'

'Come now,' said the vet, 'you've just got to face it. First of all God does not go round healing horses and second, it's a complete impossibility for bones to fix back together after they have been broken for over six weeks.'

'But the Lord has healed Jacky Boy,' I insisted, 'and it's only six weeks and one day. Surely that won't make a difference?'

'It's totally impossible. Phone me back when you're feeling more yourself. I must get on with surgery now. Goodbye.'

'Goodbye,' I said weakly, and replaced the receiver.

'Why can't that vet believe me?' I flustered. 'The Lord has healed Jacky Boy, I just know it.'

Chapter 4

The Move

Jacky Boy was not instantly healed completely. His wound was still gaping open a good eight inches and he was still lame. Yet something wonderful had definitely happened: whereas yesterday he could not walk, today he could trot; whereas yesterday you could move his shoulder joint loosely with your hand, today it was firm. As far as I was concerned, God had definitely heard my prayer and was healing my horse. I knew now, beyond doubt, that Jacky Boy would get better.

I gave him a last pat and on the way home decided to stop at the Post Office. There was a letter waiting for me from Drakensberg. I ripped it open. It was from John. It was to welcome me to the staff of the Drakensberg boys choir school and to let me know that he would be collecting my horses and me on the 30th of November. This was so that I could settle in and begin schooling some of the horses before the boys started their new year.

At last things were beginning to fit together, yet there was a lot to get done before the move, so the next two weeks just sped by.

Jacky Boy was improving all the time and soon even his large gash began to close up. When I visited him in the evenings he would sometimes trot up to me as he whinnied and though still lame, there was a steady improvement.

Before long the 30th of November arrived and I was ready and packed. My combi was already packed with the lounge suite, bed, clothing and all the saddlery. The jumps, poles and wings would be packed in the lorry behind the horses and the Sulki cart was already on top of the combi roof, with the wheels fitting down to the combi windows on both sides.

The lorry arrived on time, driven by John himself. We did not waste time: soon Gunflash, Monty and Head Hunter were loaded. Only Jacky Boy to go – he always had to be loaded last.

This time Jacky did not want to load. We coaxed with food; we then got firm; we even gave him a hiding. Nothing would work.

'Ride him in,' said John.

'I can't, he's lame,' I replied.

We struggled on another half-hour and John was losing his patience.

'If you don't get him in, in the next five minutes,' he warned, 'you will have to leave him behind.'

That really changed my mind and vaulting onto his back and firmly using both legs, he went straight in. What relief! We bolted him in, loaded the jumps and were off.

If was a good five-hour journey, and I followed behind in the grey combi. We arrived in the late afternoon to misted pastel shades of the lowering sun, casting its soft touch upon the mountain slopes and causing long shadows on all within its path. Soon the sky too began to change its colour to a soft pink, which in turn touched the valleys with its soft warm reflection.

Soon John was turning the big truck into the narrow driveway, scattering fluffy white bantam sulkies everywhere.

I jumped out the moment the lorry stopped and ran to the ramp. 'OK Jacky Boy?' I shouted. 'We're here.'

Jacky stamped his feet impatiently and John came round and pulled down the ramp. Jacky was more than ready to come out first and almost pulled me down the ramp. He was sweating a bit, but otherwise was fine. I put him into his new stable as quickly as I could and then unloaded the rest of the horses and fed them. I then got my case from the combi.

John then showed me to the cottage where I was to stay. It was beautiful. We entered through a narrow kitchen into a lounge with large wooden beams across the ceiling and a stone fireplace. Cottage type French doors opened out into the garden and the most magnificent view of the now almost dark valleys below. I then went through to the bedroom, also with French doors and full windows the full length of the bedroom.

What a joy it would be to wake up to such a view. I was filled with excitement. 'This is a paradise,' I exclaimed. 'And this cottage is just so lovely.'

'I thought you would like it,' said John, 'and I hope you will be very happy here.'

'I am sure I will be,' I replied.

John then showed me a dish of food that had been prepared for me in the kitchen and said, 'You will eat breakfast at 8.00 am in the main house. See you then,' and he was gone.

I looked around the cottage again. Yes, it was beautiful. I opened the French doors, breathed in the sweet mountain air and listened to the crickets that sounded extra loud against the silence of the mountains. Then I went to bed.

Jacky Boy – jumping after the miraculous healing

Chapter 5

The Drakensberg Boys Choir

I awoke to the sun touching my face. I leapt out of bed and went straight to the window. What a view! There were clouds below us and as you looked through a hole in the clouds you could see it was raining below the clouds. Yet here above the clouds we were in bright sunlight. 'It's like being on an island,' I thought, 'with the clouds swirling round us like the sea.'

I was so excited by the view that I got a piece of paper to record the beauty and write to my parents about it.

'This is my new home high above the clouds,' I wrote. 'It's like I've left earth, for when I look down at the clouds, knowing the dull drizzle below, I think of these mountains as an island, with the clouds swirling around below like a foaming sea with fluffy white horses gracefully flowing over the rocky peaks.'

This surely is the sunny island above the clouds, the island of heaven.

'Just right for a postcard,' I thought, and then I looked at my watch. 7.30 am. 'Well, I'd better go and feed the horses, before I go for breakfast,' and off I went.

The horses seemed pleased to see me, and even more pleased to see their food. There was a lot of work to be done. The previous people had used the deep litter system, because of a lack of bedding. This I really wanted to get stuck into replacing, as new bedding had arrived.

I then went in for breakfast. The tall Zulu girl had laid the table and was preparing an English breakfast of eggs and bacon.

'Morning madam,' she said,

'Morning,' I replied. 'What is your name?'

'Miriam,' she replied. 'How many eggs do you want, one or two?'

'Two is fine,' I replied.

John then came down the stairs and we had breakfast.

'I want you to spend the rest of December and January schooling the ponies before the boys start school,' he said. 'Breakfast, lunch and supper will be served here until school starts, after that breakfast and lunch will be served at the school.'

'That's fine,' I said.

It was now 7th December, 1975. I got to work on unloading my things, cleaning out the stables, cleaning the tack and schooling the horses. I worked mainly on the stallion and Shah the 14.2 part-Arab gelding who was rather a handful. The other horses I found to be quiet and easy for most young people to handle.

The weeks just flew by. I spent a fairly quiet Christmas with the Tungay family, then just got on with the horses and made a few improvements to the stable yard.

Soon the day arrived. I was to start work at 8.30 am at the school. The boys had arrived the night before.

It had been raining again causing the old grey combi to skid left and right on the slippery gravel roads. Turning into the road to the school was even worse. It took skill just to keep the combi on the road and the *Sound of Music* song, 'I have confidence in confidence alone' came into my head as I skidded down into the entrance to the school and literally slid into one of the parking bays.

I jumped out into the rain and ran to the main entrance of the school.

John was there. 'Follow me,' he said. 'I will introduce you and then I would like you to give them a short talk on the history of the horse.'

'OK,' I replied, with my head spinning, wondering where to start with less than five minutes preparation.

I thought, 'Now what is the programme we're to work to?

Yes, it starts with the lighting of the Olympic flame, the Romans. I will tell them how the programme that we are to work to came from the history of the horse.'

John led me into the packed dining room. Gavin and Dion immediately spotted me and began to clap which set off the whole school. John then introduced me and I nervously gave the talk, which was fairly brief, but covered the main theme.

After that I joined the teachers in the staff dining hall. There John introduced me to the teachers and then asked me to join him, his brother and mother at their table. John's mother, known as Ma, was quite a character with a strong looking face. I felt a little nervous, especially as she appeared to eye my every move. John's brother was a pleasant looking slim gentleman with a moustache and had recently got married to Linda. She had been the previous riding instructor, who I was replacing, and she too was at the table.

Everyone seemed very pleasant and as soon as breakfast was over, I went outside to wait for the eight 'national team' boys to come out, so that I could drive them up for their first lesson with me.

They came rushing out with Dion and Gavin in the lead and Taubin the red-headed boy right behind. Then came Gert, an Afrikaans farmer's son, and Martin, a more studious looking boy, Johhannes, Gerald, and the youngest Stephen.

They piled into the grey combi. I started it up and tried to drive up over the skiddy roads with as few skids as possible, with the boys singing 'Coming round the mountain'. As soon as we arrived, they jumped out and rushed the already saddled horses, almost shocking them out of their wits. I shouted 'Walk, don't scare the horses.' At least Dion and Gavin knew better and they helped me to sort out the beginners and get them onto the horses.

The lesson went slowly, with five beginners and three who could ride. There was a lot of work ahead to bring them up to standard; at least they were to ride every day.

The day went quite well with more classes that afternoon from the fifty paying riders of the school. They were not serious riders like the national team, and liked the idea of mostly out-rides into the mountains.

That night as I walked to the cottage, the full moon filtered its way down the shady mountain valleys, giving a dreamlike fairytale look, misty and soft with folding black shadows from the tall trees. What beauty surrounded me; a little lonely maybe, but happy in my work.

The weeks just flew by. I worked the boys through the basics. I introduced sitting trot before teaching them to rise to the trot. I did this because it helped to deepen and strengthen their seat positions more quickly, as we had a tight programme to work to.

In the afternoons I took the boys from the school out on hacks and slowly explored beautiful rides through the forests and up into the mountains. Then one day the boys showed me a beautiful waterfall hidden down in a canyon.

'A hermit used to live down there in a cave,' shouted one of them against the sound of the waters. 'He was a lovely old man. He used to come down to the school shop once a week for his pension and food, then one day he just got too old to walk and they took him to an old-age home, where he died a few weeks later.'

By this time we were dismounting, tying up the horses, to walk the last bit. It was a narrow, steep path, which wound its way round large rocks and trees. Old man's beard, which was a drooping green moss, hung from the trees and only a few shafts of sunlight managed to filter their way through the trees. Soon we arrived at a large pool by the side of a large cave. A tall waterfall splashed down into the pool, sending up a spray of water which formed a rainbow.

We scrambled up over the rocks and into the cave. Inside the cave were two homemade wicker chairs and a table.

'Come over here,' shouted one of the boys, running ahead to another cave within the cave. 'This was the hermit's bedroom.'

I went over, and sure enough there was a cleverly-made, wicker-type bed made from woven monkey ropes, and tied to cut logs, with woven grass over it to make a mattress. There were also a couple of old blankets in almost unusable condition. This hermit had certainly made himself quite comfortable in his cave home. We then walked round the cave and to my joy went right behind the waterfall. What a sight it was to see the wall of water falling in front of you, with the light of the sun coming right through the water to give light to the cave.

We could hardly hear each other talk for the thundering water. It was a wonderful experience of appreciating nature and all of us could see how the old man enjoyed living in this hidden paradise. We all drank from the sweet crystal-clear water, then realised we had better get back before sunset.

We rode home in silence, each with our own thoughts. Somehow the visit had given us an outlook on life from a different dimension. It was an outlook entirely from nature, like a reflection of something greater and more beautiful than any human creation could ever achieve. It was as if nature and its wild animals knew something that we didn't know. Their good health, contentment and unity with each other spoke of something quite wonderful and something I wanted to know more of.

The trip to the waterfall had made an impression on all of us. Now the boys, seeing my joy at what we saw, wanted to show me all the beautiful places. It was getting into March 1976, the hottest part of the year, and the boys told me to take a bathing costume on the next ride.

This ride was made to another waterfall in the opposite direction. This too was hidden from sight, as it had made a deep depression into the hillside and fell between cliffs into a deep pool. Here there were far fewer trees, so the sun could shine right onto the pool, and the cliffs were not that high, making it possible to dive from them.

Soon the boys were diving into the deep pool or sliding down the smooth rock into the pool with the waterfall.

The waterfall here fell on the slant of the rock and made the most perfect water slide that ducked you well under the water on reaching the pool. The boys loved it. I swam with them, but declined from diving in. We were having so much fun that we did not notice the tribe of monkeys that had come to watch us, until we heard them.

'Quick, grab your clothes,' shouted the boys. 'The monkeys will take them.'

We scrambled out of the pool and rushed for our clothes just in time, and the monkeys ran off.

The national team was coming on quite well by this time. Our biggest difficulty was the 'flags of the nations', where the boys had to ride in exact order, turn at the same time, the right distance apart, and walk in a straight line onto the centre line. Not as easy as it looks and took a lot of practice every day to achieve it.

The 'Knight' and 'Saracen' were done by Dion and Gavin and this came together easily and well. 'My Blink Vors Perd' was also an easy part with the talented Dion on his chestnut horse, Sharon and artistic Gavin dressed up as the 'Dame'. Stephen the smallest and most athletic was the best for lunging and could soon stand up at a trot, while Falcon trotted calmly round.

For the lighting of the Roman Olympics I had to teach the horses to jump fire.

'I can't do that,' I exclaimed, when John told me to do it.

'Of course you can,' replied John. 'You can teach a horse to do anything.'

'But not jump fire,' I went on. 'All animals are afraid of fire.'

'That's just what I want for our show,' he said. 'Something that will attract the audience.'

'But please, not fire,' I went on.

'Don't worry' he replied, 'I have worked it all out. Take the aluminium pole, wrap rope round it, drench the rope with some petrol and light it. Quite safe.'

'I hate fire,' I went on further. 'Please don't do it.'

'Look,' said John, 'just light the two sides of the pole first, get the horses to jump between the fire, then slowly draw the fire in until the horses jump the actual flames.'

Seeing that there was no way out, I had to go along with him, with him there to help. To my amazement we had all

Drakensberg – the chapel

Drakensberg – the national team

the horses, including my own horses Gunflash and Monty, jumping the flames as well, and the training took no more than 30 minutes to achieve. This really increased my respect for the temperament of the Arab horses, as well as my own horses.

Soon, at the drop of the flag, the boys were racing up the ménage, jumping the flames in the middle, stopping at the other end, sending their partners ('the slaves') to light their torch from the same flame and then run back to hand them the long-handled fire torch, for the boys to ride back with only one hand on the reins, jumping the wall of flames again, and light the big Olympic flame, which would burn through their whole show.

The winner would get a wreath around the horse's neck. Of course the boys loved this event as it was a real race between them, which added to the excitement of the event.

The other event the boys loved was 'The Arabian Knights'. They would dress up in Arab costumes and do a musical ride to Arab music, which ended up with three horses on each side of the arena. Then came the test for the best 'Arab' to win the Arab lady of his dreams. Here they had to gallop up with a sword and loop the lady's ring onto the sword. The first Arab to achieve this would put the ring onto the lady's finger, lift her onto the saddle and ride off into the night with her. For the actual performances they would use a girl volunteer from the audience. Again, competition came into this event, which brought it alive and made it most exciting.

The boys were working so well as a team, that I asked their headmaster if I could take them up into the Little Berg one weekend for a camp out. I was given permission to do this.

I thanked the headmaster, got into my old grey combi and decided to explore the countryside. It was 5.00 pm, a lovely time of day, when the colours of the countryside became softer with the lowering sun. I turned left at the road, drove along a bit and then decided to turn left again. This took me past some plantations and a dam before beginning to climb up towards the foothills.

All of a sudden, up on the foothills, in front of me, four palomino ponies came galloping into view along the skyline of the hill. They were beautiful. Their necks were arched and their white manes and tails seemed to flow in the wind. The one in front slowed down to a dancing trot and snorted into the wind. The next second they swirled round and galloped off, leaving a trail of dust.

Whose were those beautiful ponies? I got out of the combi. Maybe that man will know, so I walked up towards him.

'Excuse me. Who owns those palomino ponies?'

'Those ponies are wild,' he answered. 'No one can catch them. The master in the wood and thatch cottage owns them, but he can't catch them. They are very wild, no good ponies. Too clever.'

'Thank you,' I replied.

I got back into the car and drove up the hill to the wood cottage with the thatch roof and parked by some pigsties. A lady came out.

'Can I help you?' she inquired.

'Yes. I saw your palomino ponies and I wondered whether you would like to sell any of them.'

'Sell them!' she exclaimed. 'We have never even been able to touch them. We bought Sonskien (Afrikaans for sunshine) the stallion plus a filly foal eight years ago, put them on the hill and have never been able to catch them after that. Since then the filly has grown up and had two foals. One is three years old and the other is two years old. The youngest one died as a foal. Anyway, my husband will be home soon so come in for some tea and you can talk to him about them.'

I followed her into the most quaint stone and wood cottage with indigenous wood beams and the rich smell of thatch. Almost everything had been hand-made, even the wooden furniture.

'This is really lovely!' I exclaimed. 'And what a magnificent view.'

Glass patio doors opened up into a beautifully kept and artistically designed garden, heralded by the Drakensberg

Mountains themselves on the one side and overlooking the valleys on the other side. The simplicity of this lovely home contrasted by the magnificence of these mountains made me feel that this surely must be a taste of heaven.

I turned back into the home. On the walls were hanging beautiful branches of dried flowers. The lounge furniture was wood and wicker chairs and a little coffee table that had been tastefully hand-painted with flowers and varnished over. Even the picture frames on the walls looked as if they were hand-made. I loved it.

She brought in some tea and tennis biscuits and we sat down. I asked her about this beautiful home.

'Oh,' she said, 'we bought this piece of land some years ago. We had no money, so my husband and I decided to build ourselves and this is the outcome.'

'The outcome could not be better,' I replied. 'I wish I could do something like this.'

'Come, I'll show you around.'

I got up and followed.

'This is my daughter's room.'

I saw a patchwork quilt on her bed, woven grass light shades, an old pine dressing table with a soft pink teddy on it, and a woven grass mat on the wooden plank floorboards that had been sanded and polished.

The stonework was rough, made from stone and rocks they had found on the farm. This had made the wall of about three-quarters of the outside and wood poles had completed the remainder. All was so artistically done, that it could have come out of a fairytale book. No paint had been used at all and it was not needed either, for the way it was done was much more attractive.

A tall man then entered the cottage.

'This is my husband.' She introduced me and we went back into the lounge.

'Ah, so you are interested in my ponies,' he said. 'That's if you can catch them. I'll give you a deal,' he went on. 'My wife is afraid of horses. She won't get on one, not even for a fur coat. If you can catch my ponies, break the stallion and the mare in, and teach my wife and two children to ride them, then you can have the two fillies as payment. Is that a deal?' He stretched out his hand to me.

'Yes, that's a deal,' I answered, and we shook hands on it.

I was thrilled. What a challenge! Next day, after work, I went over to see how I could catch the ponies. There was a paddock, a garage for a stable and, yes, also a narrow place where hopefully I could herd them.

The following day was my day off, so asking if I could use one of their men, I tried to herd them in. This was disastrous, for though we found the ponies and we were able to herd them into the right direction, the stallion simply ran into the paddock, straight across it and jumped out the other side, with the mare right behind. Only the two fillies had been caught, which we herded into the garage, complete with bedding and water, and shut the door on them.

Every day after that, I spent my lunch-times trying to make friends with the fillies and left food out for the mare and stallion, who had not ventured too far away from the fillies. One day we were able to shut the gate on them and they were caught.

The next step was to come up three times a day to feed them. We placed the food so that they had to eat close to us, and then later only out of our hands. It worked, and very soon we were able to actually touch them and even to get them to follow us for food.

Then came the time to fit halters on them, which we did with the help of food and plenty of stroking. Once on, we left them to get used to the feel of them, before trying to lead them.

To teach them to lead we simply used food and a lead rope, rewarding them with food for responding to the pressure of the lead rope to move forwards and to stop.

Soon all the ponies were halter trained and I then concentrated on training the mare and stallion, leaving the two fillies to grow and simply to become tamer.

Chapter 6

Trip Up the Mountains

Back at school the weekend allocated for the trip up the mountains had arrived. The boys were really excited. They had planned everything – that is food and drink of course. My problem was how to carry it all, as my saddlebags were simply not big enough. Sleeping bags, rolled up in ground sheets were strapped across each pommel, horse feed was put into the sacks and tied to either side of one saddle. We then did the same on other saddles for the dry foods and extra clothing needed, eventually fitting everything on.

The nine of us at last set off, looking as if we were going for at least a month.

'Wow, keep at a walk Gavin,' I shouted. 'We have a long way to go today.'

'Do we have to?' he replied.

'Yes.'

Soon we left the gravel road and took a path up through a forest, passing a lake on our right. We then turned onto the narrow path which took us around the old man's head – a dangerously narrow path below the great rock that looked like an old man's head. Here my horse, Shah, always walked very close to the edge, which never ceased to worry me. Half the boys were also worried and were already dismounting. For safety reasons I told them all to dismount and dismounted myself, just in case the extra things we were carrying caused a problem.

Soon we were round it, remounted and on our way again, the boys now chatting contentedly amongst themselves.

My thoughts now turned to the beauty of the area that we were riding through. The path led us through little crags away from the sunlit path down to its winding streams.

Here, old and gnarled, and draped with old man's beard, the trees concealed their private secrets from the sun above. Yet somehow the sun did manage to peep through their draping shawls of greenery, lighting up sunny patches of water like hidden jewels, invading the life below those protecting trees, sending shadows across monkey ropes, logs and creeping moss.

My eyes returned to look ahead at the path winding its way through the tunnel of greenery to the bright light of the sun at the end. From one wonder to the next; for as we came out of the tunnel onto the side of the mountain we saw the snow-capped peak of the next towering mountain.

This was Cathkin peak in all its glory. What extravagant beauty! Soon the path led us onto the plateau of its little berg and a herd of a buck startled our horses.

'Hold them in!' I commanded, as the boys struggled to regain control. That, in turn, scared the buck and they were off, leaping as they went.

We rode on a little further and then stopped to have some lunch by some rocks that we used as a table. We threaded the reins through the throat lashes and tied the end of the reins to the stirrups, so that the horses could graze. Silver, the stallion, we held.

Fifteen minutes later, we remounted and made our way off the plateau and around Cathkin peak. Here we crossed another stream with a waterfall above us and then rounded the mountain into a steep valley with a river rushing down the middle of it. Luckily, though it sounded like rushing waters, it was only a foot deep and the horses were able to cross it.

Now for the last stretch, round the next mountain to the stable caves, which were actually caves on the side of the mountains.

From this mountain, one was able to look down on the magnificent view of the valleys below, where civilization carried on its way.

My mind went into thought. I was inspired by the beauty and freedom. Surely we were in search of the dream or something. We wandered on:

Wander high, wander free
Wander on in search of a dream
We had searched the world
For truth and happiness in vain
We had come to the conclusion therefore
It was no longer more than a dream
Yet we carried on searching.

We look far down upon the earth
A spire of smoke lifts silently
From a valley dreaming below
While under a veil of blue haze
The lands meet into the distant skies.

It looks so peaceful
But how peaceful is it?
What goes on down there?
Under the rule of man?

Schools carry on, Africans plough
Babies cry, old men argue
Each farm in the distance
Has its own story to tell
Of troubles and happiness
Hardships and pleasures
But what ever may happen
The world carries on.

We turn for this mountainous land
And as we do, a whistling breeze
Whispers promises of what is ahead.

Ride on, along a dusty winding path
Deep into rugged mountains, we ride
The lowering sun still shines
Sending ghostly shadows that spread
And creep up lonely peaks.

A crack of thunder echoes
Grasses rustle eerily
Cold shivers rush up your spine
A little nervous, we carry on.

We move steadily on, round the mountain
Past baboons and another crag
We feel exhausted now, but on we go
As we round the berg our hearts leap
Ahead is a valley of incredible beauty
Stretching between the mountain slopes
That reach to the skies in majestic splendour
Buck gallop in the distance, wild and free
Waterfalls sparkle like a million jewels
And old gnarled trees stand their ground.

This is the uninhibited land of beauty
So wild and free, so massive
So different from the world below
Problems come with wind rain and storm
Pleasures come with peace and beauty
Freedom and happiness, so simple so pure
Under the rule of nature
So unchanged through the centuries
Yet they ever change
Suddenly our dream has come true
But not in what we see
What we were seeking
Was not in study or in science
Art or society, but in something far greater
God is the creator of these lands too
Can He also be our Lord and security?
As He is for the animals here,
  that He cares for?
Can we yield ourselves to Him
  and by doing so find truth and happiness?
This need no longer be a dream
Can it be real and everlasting?

'Suzanne! Just look!' exclaimed Gavin.

'Are we there yet?' called Steven. 'How much further?'

'This is fantastic! Where are the caves?'

'I don't know,' I replied. 'They are supposed to be on the side of this mountain. Here, look at the map.'

I unfolded a grubby map and studied it.

'A bit further on, there should be a path up to the left of this mountain which then turns to the right and they should be somewhere along there.'

We rode on and sure enough found the path. We rode up it and then turned right as the map said, but we could not find the caves. We rode until the path petered out to nothing, so we turned round and rode back – still no caves.

'Dismount,' I ordered. 'Stephen, Gert and you hold the horses. We had better look on foot. Right, half of us look below the path,' I said, pointing at three boys, 'and we three will look above the path.'

We searched for almost fifteen minutes and I was getting worried as it was beginning to get dark.

Suddenly Touben's shrill voice came echoing round the bushes. 'I've found them!'

Sure enough, he had found them. All the boys scrambled to collect the horses and then led them over very rough ground, up a very steep slope and right into the caves.

Then came the next problem: the stable, as such, was only large enough for three horses and we had nine with us.

'Tie Silver to the other side of the caves and tie Shoron and Falcon with him. Put the geldings in the stable and the other three we will just let loose. They won't leave the rest.'

Soon every boy was busy – sorting out the horses, filling the bucket from the spring next to the caves, lighting a fire in the middle of the caves for cooking, and deciding where to lay out the sleeping bags.

The excitement! The adventure!

'Now,' said Gavin, 'I'm doing the cooking, so, Sue, leave it to us, we want to do everything.'

I was just glad that the thunder seemed to be subsiding and that we had found the caves. I left them to it and sorted out

Drakensberg – mountains unveiling themselves through the cloud

Drakensberg – the trip up to stable caves

my own horse and sleeping bag, and made sure that a few candles were lit. I was so glad that these boys were tough and not afraid. They were not just cloistered choirboys with pale angelic faces, but tough and physically active, with strength of character and initiative. Yes, the Durban newspaper was right in their heading 'Angels in boots', or as Mr Pearse said, 'Their singing was pure and immaculate, their harmonising a quality as rare and refreshing as this exhilarating air and as effortless as the flight of the eagle.'

Soon all was done, and the candles blown out. The silvery light of the half-moon shone stealthily through the trees into the caves where we were sleeping, and the sound of the jackal was heard in the distance.

We awoke just as the sun was about to come up. Dressing quickly, we ran round the base of the mountains to watch it rise from across the lands.

> 'Slanting rays of sunlight,
> adorn the lifting clouds,
> showing forth its light,
> misted truth unfolds.
>
> The new day approaches,
> upon the darkened world,
> showing forth its glory,
> of promises foretold.

I put my pen away. What did the others think of it? It was already getting hot.

'Well, that was worth the run,' one said.

'I'm hungry,' said another.

'That was really brilliant,' said Gavin.

'Race you back to the caves,' shouted another.

'I want breakfast. Hope the monkeys haven't got it by now,' I replied.

That really made them run.

Soon, out of breath, we were back in the caves. No monkeys! That was good and we all shared the tasks. Gavin was cook, of course. Dion and Touben collected wood and Gert and the others did the horses.

I then took two empty water buckets to fetch water for the horses. The spring was a few metres on from the caves, where it trickled straight out of the side of the mountain, over its little ledge and spilled about two metres into a little pool of water. All I had to do was to sit the bucket under the water and wait for it to fill up. That took a good ten minutes, so I simply sat down and waited.

It was then that I noticed the most beautiful little purple water lily – not a mark on it. I can work all my life to do something and I know it won't be perfect. No art is perfect. In fact, nothing that man can do is perfect and yet, this little water lily, far from civilisation and never touched by a human, is perfect. 'I'm going to bring my camera with me next time. I want a photo of this.'

Soon the buckets were full and I carried them back to the caves. Steven and Martin went to fetch the next buckets.

Gavin had cooked a good breakfast of eggs and baked beans on bread and butter. After that we saddled up, filled the saddlebags and mounted. Soon we were on our way home.

Chapter 7

A Mountain Top Experience

The crow trips in its path. Tommy pecks at the offending pebble and flies to a car roof. All is peaceful there, and he looks around. Some cows are walking along the road below and a calf is sniffing the nose of a young pup. A fly is buzzing round him in the sun. Tommy pecks at it and swallows it whole.

From the classroom the drone of children at work is heard. In fact, everything is incredibly peaceful. The turkeys are hidden from sight and Tommy wonders where his large friends are. He then dreams away in the sun ... no cigarettes to chew up today ... no interesting looking letters to open ... What a bore! What should he do with that lighter he stole yesterday? Surely one day his hiding place will be found.

Suddenly Tommy leaps with fright, his wings spread for flight, then relaxes as he sees the cause of the bang and clucking of turkeys. John's mum is chasing them out of the minister's lounge with a ruler and slams the door behind them. 'Oh well,' thinks Tommy, 'glad it wasn't me this time.'

The days began to get busier and busier. I had the National Team to work seriously with at 9.00 am every morning, as the tour was drawing closer. Then I taught the seven students, gave them their lectures, had lunch and then had fifty pupils spread out from Monday to Friday with two classes of five each day. At least the weekends were still free at times, when we were not at horse shows.

The horse shows had also gone well. The boys had done well at the Newcastle Show. Gavin got a 4th on Shah in the

Dressage championships and also did well in the jumping. Dion had a 1st and 2nd on Silver Leaf, the Stallion, and I had a 1st in the jumping and, like Gavin, a 4th in Dressage. We had also gone to a few smaller shows where we had done well.

All this time I had tried to fit in a day to go up into the mountains again, and at last found one, only two months before the tour.

This time I had to go alone. For this reason I left as early as possible on Shah in order to arrive back before dark.

Shah and I headed straight for Champagne Castle. We had all day to appreciate the beauty of the mountains and think.

Champagne Castle stands adorned in sunlight. Round her peaks a necklace of cloud folds and shines in the sun, like cultured pearls. She towers up through the clouds appearing above them like a castle of the skies.

Her waterfalls spill down her rocky face, like sparkling champagne, to reach her heart within her rolling green valleys, from where she stands throned by the little berg to keep watch over the hazy lands of Natal.

Soon we were up onto her little berg and made our way round the side of the mountain to the stable caves.

As soon as I arrived at the caves, I took my camera to take a photo of the water lily, but it was withered and dead. I took a photo of it anyway, as I had carried the camera all that way and without staying much longer, rode back to the school in order to get back before dark. This was the first time I had gone out alone, and there was a sense of fear in riding this far. Anything could happen.

The students also wanted a chance of a night in the mountains before the end of their three-month course, which would end just before the tour. So again I planned a weekend for the trip.

They were not quite as tough as the boys, and the girls moaned about their seat bones quite quickly. By the time we had reached the caves Claudia and Nicky were quite exhausted and, after unsaddling the horses, immediately had a rest while I went to fetch water from the spring.

To my amazement there were three beautiful purple water lilies – just as perfect, not a flaw, not a speck. I sank down into a heathery seat to admire them, simply to admire them.

Just then it was as if I heard a voice; whether outward or inward, I cannot tell, but the words I will never forget.

'As that water lily had to die of itself, for its seeds to break open and new life to emerge, so I died on the cross, that many may have new life in Me.'

I looked around – nothing. I looked at the water lilies, still and silent. All of a sudden, for the first time, I understood. 'So Jesus died on the cross to break the power of sin and death and rose on the third day, that we mere humans could have new life in Him?'

'Lord, Jesus.' I whispered. 'Can even I have this new life too?'

At that moment beautiful warmth came right into me. I was open to it. I wanted it. Was Jesus touching me? Can this be, this wonderful?

'Lord,' I whispered again. 'I give my life to You. You are real. You are true, and from this moment on, I want to live for You.'

I felt enveloped with His glorious love. I had found truth; I had found what I had been searching so long for.

I sat there a long time; I did not want to leave. I began to listen to all the mountain sounds:

> Listen to the whispering breeze
> Blowing gliding mists over hidden valleys
> Listen to the drop of water
> as it drips from within the cave
> Listen to the sound of birds
> as they chatter on below the mists
> Listen to that chirping cricket
> as it calls to its hidden mate
> Listen quietly to all
> and suddenly you become part of it
> Part of the beauty of God's love.

All of a sudden I felt different. Never had I felt pure enough to be part of the beauty of God's love, but Jesus had cleaned me. I confessed my sin anyway, but it appeared that the moment He touched me, I was clean, I was pure, and I was part of the beauty of God's love. I was filled with incredible joy and peace. This was right now the most glorious moment of my life.

I wanted to leap for joy, to fly with the music of the winds, to swing with the joy of freedom, but I had two buckets of water to get back to the cave. Oh, this indescribable joy! I picked up the two buckets and made it to the cave at a walk.

'You took a long time,' commented Claudia.

'What's happened to you?' remarked Debbie. 'You look so happy. You're face is shining.'

'I'll tell you sometime,' I answered. 'Is Jeff back with the wood yet?'

It was getting cold as winter was on the way. We built a fire, ate supper and crawled into our sleeping bags. The girls were still cold, so I gave them my rug to share.

It was a very cold night, for my sleeping bag was not a good one and of all nights it went below freezing and puddles from the recent rains froze over.

About 2.00 am I could not stand the cold so I got up, got onto Shah's back and put the sleeping bag and sheepskin saddle over us. Shah did not mind at all and just stood quietly. I am sure I was keeping him warm as well.

At the first sign of dawn, I was up and leaving the others sleeping, went round the base of the mountain to get a view of the rising sun.

A New Day

Awaken to dawn; watch the sun rise from across the lands
Sending its warm rays of light, that awakens the new day and melts the ice.
As one watches, the cold heart warms to the beauty of the cheerful yellow beams
that sprawl across the ice, conquering all darkness.

The cold of the night, causing waters to ice solid has ended,
the darkness binding things to a standstill has gone,
as light triumphantly brings the world back to a bright new day.
Sunrise is like a symbol of God, showing the dark world into this glorious light.
Oh awaken to dawn of a new day, a new life in the light of the Lord.
Allow his loving rays of light, to hold you up,
to guide the way through this darkened world.

Yes, this was the first day of the rest of my life as a Christian. Everything seemed to speak of God, the sunrise, the birds, nature, everything. This was wonderful, to at last understand, for life at last to make sense.

Chapter 8

On Tour

Coming down from those mountains, yes, in one sense was coming back down to earth. Yet, in another sense, I was still floating on air.

There was a new excitement, a new joy, a glow in my heart and a peace that passes all understanding. Something wonderful had definitely happened to me. So much so that I decided to go to church the following Sunday. Yes, and by horse and cart.

I harnessed Monty to the trap and drove him merrily down the gravel road, down the S-bend, past the Boys School and another half-mile to the Elmiridal Hotel, where the chapel was situated. I then tied Monty up, gave him his hay net and entered the thatch-roofed chapel. I hadn't been in a church for years.

The service was very traditional and the view of Champagne Castle through the large arched windows was magnificent.

After the service I stayed a while to share with the minister what had happened to me and asked him about the Holy Spirit that the book of Corinthians spoke about.

'Oh that,' he said, 'was only for the twelve Apostles, not for people of today.'

I felt my heart sink, thanked him and made my way back to Monty.

'How can you put a horse in a cart?' asked a little lady. 'Quite cruel I say,' she went on.

I took no notice, patted Monty, untied him and got into the trap and quietly drove him home.

I felt confused, yet the glow was still within me. Either I was crazy, or what the Bible said was true. The Bible seemed to have confirmed that the experience I had on the mountain was true, yet a trained man of God seemed to think otherwise. Surely I was not the only person who has had an experience like that today? Surely God has touched others, like He touched me? If only I could meet one. 'Meanwhile,' I decided, 'I believe, and I will carry on believing. I will follow, even if I am the only person in the world and everyone thinks I'm mad, I will still follow Jesus like the Bible says. I will carry on reading it. It seemed more exciting than the sermon was. Man always managed to make anything seem dull, even in these magnificent mountains.

Anyway, the tour was drawing very near. Every morning we practised the programme. The flags of the nations took up most of the time, as any drill ride would. Riding with only one hand on the reins, while holding up a large flag with the right hand was not the easiest thing to do. Weight aids had to be used more effectively, especially if a horse managed to loosen the rein that was held in the left hand, which resorted to a neck rein instead to turn or complete a circle.

The day finally arrived; tack polished, horses well groomed and ready, costumes packed in large blue trunks. Every boy packed and ready.

The horse lorry had also arrived and needed to be turned around to face the road before loading the horses. This was not easy, as there was hardly any room to turn on the sloping ground.

Suddenly the wheels caught some wood and the whole lorry fell over on its side. We all ran to see if the driver was OK, which fortunately he was.

'What now?' asked the boys.

'I don't know. I'll ask John,' and ran inside to phone him.

'I'll send up the school tractor and some ropes,' he replied.

About half-an-hour later the tractor arrived and we watched as the tractor actually did manage to pull the lorry back onto its wheels again. Quite a scary operation to watch. The damage? Only one dent. Would it start? Believe it or not, first time!

We loaded up the eight horses, the boys climbed into the minibus and we finally left nearly two hours late.

Our first town was called Ermello. We went straight to the sports field and unloaded the horses for a final groom before the show. The boys were nervous, but there was no time for nerves, as we still had a lot to do.

John connected up all the sound systems and erected the roped pole for the first event – the lighting of the torch for the night, which was to be done by the Romans.

The minutes were rushing by and people began to arrive. The horses were tied up and the boys were rummaging in the tin trunk to line up their costumes for the show.

'Can't find my Roman shoes,' blurted Stephen, the youngest.

I went to help find the missing sandal.

'Get onto your horses,' I told the others. 'Stephen, get onto Falcon. I'll find it.'

John was on his organ and the moonlight gave off a misted glow on the sports field. Someone was already lighting the petrol soaked rope around the pole, apparently having a struggle to do so.

'Here's your sandal on the grass. Here, Stephen, let me tie it on.'

'Ladies and Gentlemen, the lighting of the torch at the Olympic games by the Romans.'

'Hurry. Go!'

The boys now cantered in and made a rather untidy line up. The other team with their partners, 'The Slaves', stood at the other end of the marked out arena. The fire pole, now lit and giving off some black smoke, was across the middle. Each rider held up an unlit torch, the flag was dropped and they were off at a gallop towards the fire jump. Dion and Silver Leaf were first to clear the jump, Falcon refused; Gavin got Sharon over, followed by Sharida and Shah. Ryad and Falcon were turned round and had another go. Falcon gave an enormous jump and Stephen landed in front of the saddle, but rode on regardless, with Reid galloping behind, despite the slaves with unlit torches already running towards them to light their torches from the fire. The boys ran back from the fire with high-flaming torches, lifted them to the riders, who were off, riding at the jump again with one hand on the reins and one hand holding the torch. The audience were getting excited, as at night the flames of the fire looked even larger as the horses and riders jumped through the flames. No refusals this time and the first rider in managed to light the large torch which would burn for the remainder of the evening. Gavin on Sharon was the winner and the wreath was put on Sharon's neck to the sound of triumphant music. What a start to the show! The audience rose from their seats to clap.

Next came the flags of the nations, the drill ride that had taken so much practice. It went off quite well, though rather tame after the first item. That was followed by the tales of the Arabian knights, another exciting performance, as the knights had to race to get a ring off the hanging pole for the damsel. Dion had the great joy of winning and sweeping a volunteer girl from the audience onto his stallion, cantered out of the arena in triumph.

The last item was little Stephen, on the lunge on Falcon at a canter. Yes, he did manage a shaky stand once round a circle, while the audience cheered him on, until lifting his legs out sideways, he landed back on Falcon's back with a bit of a bump. But he had made it.

There was a rush in the interval to get the knight and Saracen ready for battle. The battle provided an exciting start to the rest of the evening, until one rider was pushed off his horse as dead and carried out on a stretcher pretending to be really dead. This was followed by a duet of Gavin and myself; Gavin on Falcon dressed in his red riding jacket and myself side-saddle on Shah to show the rise of dressage. We worked well together, showing off some lateral work and an extended trot, which got applause, and finishing with Shah in Piaffe and a Lavade. Shah was the only horse I had ever

How your gift helps

IN GREAT BRITAIN

Caring for the needy at 32 community centres

Providing for the elderly in 40 eventide homes

Housing over 5,000 homeless men, women and families

Protecting deprived youngsters in 10 residential homes

Re-uniting families — 5,000 investigations each year

AND AROUND THE WORLD

The Army is at work in 89 countries using 126 languages

Providing shelter for over 30,000 homeless people in over 600 hostels

Giving jobs to over 18,000 people in 215 industrial homes

Training 1,300 people at 17 special centres

Feeding the hungry at 166 distribution points

Fighting fatal diseases in third world countries

Educating 252,500 children in over 1,000 schools

'May this Christmas bring
to you the joy you give to others
with your kindness...'

THE SALVATION ARMY

managed to train to that level and that was thanks to the Major who invited me onto his Lipizzaner team for a year.

'Here come the Basutos' followed. Then came a comedy called 'My blink vorsperd', an African legend about a boy showing off his beautiful chestnut to a pretty girl. She drops her hanky and asks Dion to dismount and pick it up for her, then suddenly she vaults onto his horse and gallops off into the distance.

The 'Epilogue – the Horse' ended the concert, and then we were off to pack up our belongings, see to the horses and go to the homes of the various families who put us up for the night.

The rest of the tour went almost as well as the first night, with the boys getting more practised each night.

Piet Ratief was an interesting town. I had to ride the whole team through the small town to advertise our show. I rode in front side-saddle on Shah, and the others rode two-by-two, each holding a flag of a nation. After thirty minutes of trotting through the town, it was quite hard to keep the large flags upright, but somehow we did manage.

That night the wind came up and it was difficult for the boys to clear the fire which was blowing towards them, so there were more refusals than usual. After the race some of the grass caught fire and there was a rush to get the fire fully out. I felt that we had taken a risk there and possibly should have cancelled the first item, but the audience seemed to enjoy the extra excitement anyway. I was also invited to come and give a riding course there.

Vryhied was also a very nice town, though some of the boys went down with flu and struggled to give a good show. On the second night John also had flu and kept being sick, so I had to take over the mike. I had never done this before and was extremely nervous – especially with the boys sick and having to do things alone. Occasionally they came in a little late and I had to think up things to say.

Soon it was the interval.

John had taken some tablets and he said, 'Suzanne, you go and get ready for the duet, I think I can take over now.'

I was very relieved.

After the knight and Saracen act, Dion and I entered on Falcon and Shah with floodlights blazing down. Our horses danced to the music of Mozart's first symphony – light and springy, elegant in the collected trot, quarters lowered, forehand light, necks arched, ears pricked, they trotted in time to the music, then turned in and halted.

'Side-saddle on Shah is Suzanne Ratcliffe, our chief instructor, and astride is Gavin Blunt, one of her pupils,' came over the loudspeaker. We saluted and the clapping echoed out. It was a good turn out, 800 at least.

We trotted on, tracked left and keeping together turned down the centre line. At X we went into leg yielding away from each other. Shah was going well in time to the music and we soon completed the show and were asked to repeat the extended trot in which Shah floated across the ground. I was thrilled.

Suddenly over the mike, John announced that because half the boys and himself were suffering from flu, he had cancelled the shows in the last two towns and was going to return home the next day for proper medical attention. Though sensible, this was bad news, and caused sadness to me and the boys.

Following the Basutus and the comedy, came the 'Epilogue – the Horse'. Riders in red coats filed in on their Arabs. Steven led the grey Stallion, Silver Leaf. They turned in, halted and saluted. Gavin then dismounted and took the mike. The organ was playing 'Fill the world with love', and Gavin's voice came over clearly and softly as he spoke the words of the epilogue poem with much feeling.

All of a sudden I felt tears running down my face. I thought back to the fun we had preparing this show, and the boys' happy voices and singing echoing out of my grey combi as I drove them back to school. I recalled the shows we had been to, the boys' rosettes flapping gaily on the front window of the horsebox ... the way they took down their notes during lectures without a sound ... their beautifully neat books, a pleasure to look at ... their naughtiness too, when they decorated Mike's car like a wedding car ... and simply playing the fool.

'There is nothing more powerful . . . ' Gavin went on.

He spoke beautifully, I thought, and what an actor he is . . . the fun and laughter of the audience when they did 'My Blink Vorsperd Bit', which means 'my chestnut horse' in Afrikaans.

I love these boys and they have been a pleasure to work with and a credit in the few weeks of riding they have done with me. Surely this is not our last show. What would tomorrow bring?

The poem ended, 'Ladies and Gentleman, the Horse.'

Some of the audience were really touched, I noticed, and as John played the National Anthem the audience rose to attention. When it ended the clapping echoed out.

I wiped my tears. These boys had put on a good show again. I hoped it wouldn't be the last – they deserved more than that.

Drakensberg – a scene from the 'Singing Horsement'

Chapter 9

New Horizons

Arriving home seemed to be quite an anticlimax after the excitement of the tour and the hard work preparing it.

I spent more time with the palomino ponies that were now very tame and taught the two children to ride them, which they greatly enjoyed. Now it was mum's turn. She had already been watching her children have their lessons, so why not at least get on? I took Son Skyn to a bench, helped her to mount and then led her slowly round. I repeated this, and day by day she improved until she could ride them on her own, and was able to walk, trot and canter.

Her husband kept his promise. He was thrilled for her and gave me the two fillies, which thrilled me.

The older three-year-old pony I called 'High Blest' because she was blessed with every good quality a pony could wish for. The two-year-old I named 'High Light', because when she moved she was so light on her feet that she never seemed to touch the ground at all.

I was even more excited to bring the two ponies up to our farm and put them out with Jacky Boy, Monty and Gunflash. They all got on well. Jacky Boy had been completely sound for a long time now, but I had given him a long rest anyway.

We also went to a couple more horse shows and I did two weekend courses.

Christmas came and passed, as did a couple of out of season storms. The children had returned to school after their six-week holidays and we were to plan our next year. However TV had just arrived in South Africa and everyone became a TV fan. Whole villages would go up a hill where they could get good reception, watching the TV from tents and fold-up chairs, sometimes even in rain. This worried John, as he wondered if people would still want to watch our shows.

Today was 15th February and there seemed to be an almost deathly silence after the recent storms. The hills were hazy and the mountains in the distance were in a blue hazy mist. The tall grasses seemed almost without movement and the occasional call of a bird cut through the still air, breaking the silence for a brief moment.

Why so quiet? I listened – there was a bee buzzing in the distance, a man was pushing a wheelbarrow. I listened, and the sounds came to me. To notice things you have just to listen.

A cow was mooing, trees rustled almost silently in the gentle breeze, and more birds were speaking their minds in the distance.

Yet I had a feeling within of sadness and frustration: sadness for John, his school, his horses, the boys, his fairy-tale dreams. I had heard via the grapevine that John was going to sell and move the riding school from here and set up a new place somewhere down in the valley. I loved it up here; I did not want to go anywhere else.

But what I had heard was true and the next day John took me to see the new premises – a barn, no arena and shared accommodation with other school staff.

At the same time I had received through the post invitations to teach weekend courses: another one in Vrghied and a new one in Barkly East. Soon the dates were set.

Vrghied was close by, only two-and-a-half hour's drive, but the Mossips still wanted to put me up in their home. This was lovely, as they lived on a sheep farm.

It was about 5.30 on Friday afternoon when I arrived at the farm. Mrs Mossip came out of her farmhouse to meet me.

'When did it happen?' she exclaimed.

'Nothing happened,' I said, confused.

'Yes it has,' she replied. 'When did you become a Christian?'

'How do you know that I have become a Christian?' I replied, amazed.

'I can see it on your face. Do come in and tell me all about it. I'm a Christian too.'

It was wonderful to be able at last to share with someone all that had happened and Enid joined in too, as we talked late into the night.

The next morning we were up at 6.00, and Enid took me for a ride up into the hills on her Palomino ponies fitted with Western saddles. Riding with such long stirrups and long reins was a new experience for me. Once up the hill, Enid got off and took a photo of me on her horse with the sun slowly rising above the hills. It was a wonderful ride.

We had twelve riders on the course, divided into two groups of six and joined together for the lectures. There were two lessons and a lecture in the morning, and the same in the afternoon. On the Sunday afternoon there was an exam which six entered and passed the elementary riding certificate. It was a really good and busy weekend.

The following weekend was the Barkly East course. This was quite a distance away, a good five-hour drive, and so Mike offered to come with me for the drive.

We were put up in rooms in the local hotel. The next morning Mike and I met for breakfast and then went out promptly at 8.00 am to wait to be picked up. To our surprise we were not only met by a car, but were led back to the show grounds by eight horses, trotting two-by-two ahead of the car.

The Riding Club had sixteen riders and horses waiting. I split them up into the normal two groups with the better riders in one group and the rest in the other, and we met together for the lectures.

The horses were an interesting mix: from very unschooled to American saddle bred show horses that were fully 5 gaited. The saddles were also interesting: a semi-military saddle, an Australian stock saddle, a couple of Lane Fox show saddles for gaited horses, a Western saddle and English saddles. Bridles were anything from curbs to snaffles. Lectures and advice on the correct saddlery for the horses all took some sorting out. The riders were very keen though, and by that afternoon some of the saddlery had been replaced by new, after a two-hour drive to the nearest saddle and feed merchants.

In the afternoon they brought me a horse that only walked or cantered. It could not, or would not, trot. I got on and after about fifteen minutes had the horse trotting. They were very excited about this and asked me if I would come and set up a riding school in Barkly East. I said I would think about it, and carried on with the course which went very well. Soon all was over and we returned to the school.

It was barely a week later when a letter arrived from Barkly East. They were actually serious about offering me the job and had gone to the town council. They had agreed to give me free of charge the use of the show ground stables, club house and arena if I would start up and run a riding school in their town with the hope of attracting more tourists there.

I phoned Mike about it and he thought I should take it.

'After all,' he said, 'running your own riding school will put you on your own feet, rather than working for such a low salary at the Drakersberg Boys Choir School.'

Also the move down the hill and sharing with everyone else was not attractive. It was, however, going to be painful leaving the boys and these beautiful mountains, but at least Barkly East was still in the mountains.

After a little more consideration I accepted the job and gave in my notice to John. He was not too happy about it, but very understanding and wished me well.

Chapter 10

Barkly East

It was hard saying goodbye to the boys.

'Please come and see us when you have time,' they called out to us.

'I will,' I shouted back. 'I promise.' And I meant it.

Soon my old lorry with all the horses and belongings loaded on was on its way with Mike driving, as I still had no heavy-duty licence. I had to follow in my combi and with Mike's friend in his car so that he could get back to school.

It was a long, tedious journey following the big black horsebox. 'I hope I am doing the right thing,' I thought. I had not even prayed about it.

Sunset was approaching and we were following along by a river's edge. I looked to see . . .

Bleak scenery passing unnoticed – but hold still, look again, see what you are missing. Watch those graceful weeping willows sweep along the river banks like ballerinas. Watch the reflection of the crimson skies ripple in the calm waters. The stillness, the peace. A wild duck swoops across the valley and gracefully cuts through the waters, sending ripples out to the waters edge. 'That's what we do to the Lord,' I said aloud. 'We miss His love and beauty, we let Him go unnoticed.' I had accepted the Lord into my heart and yet could let Him go unnoticed. I had not even prayed about a decision as big as this. Was I leaving the boys and the happiness of the mountains for promotion and money? I hoped not. Was I listening to the advice of man, rather than my own heart, or the leading of God? I hoped not.

But there was no turning back now. We descended down

the last road in Natal and into the Transkie. It was dark now and the road was full of pot-holes as we drove past little kraals of mud brick with thatched roofs and small plantations of mielies. The only light was candlelight, flickering through the small windows that didn't even have any glass.

After three hours we began to climb the next mountain range into the Eastern Cape, and an hour after that arrived at Barkly East. We turned into the show grounds at almost 11.00 pm. Mike helped me unload the horses, put them into the stables, give them water and lucerne, and then said good-bye, as he wanted to get back to the school as soon as possible.

I opened the door of the caravan that was waiting for me close to the stables, lit the gas lamp and brought in the main things from the horsebox. It was very cold, so I decided to go straight to bed.

The dawn awoke me. It was icy cold, so I got up early to sort out my belongings and feed the horses. Everything felt very cold and lonely.

Mrs Molenzee arrived at 10.00 am and welcomed me. She had at least sixteen pupils for me, mostly from the previous course, so I would know them. As she had to get back to work, she then left.

During the day I found out where to buy horse feed, bought some groceries and settled in.

That evening six of the potential pupils came to see me and booked lessons. My new life began from there, and during the next month I built up to twenty-three pupils a week, which was not really sufficient. I was also invited onto the town committee and was asked to help design some tourist brochures, which was quite enjoyable. I was also taken around the tourist sites, to help me with the design. They also asked me what I needed to build a riding school on the land next to the show grounds. They would do the building and then rent me the building and land on a ninety-nine year lease at a very low rent. This sounded fantastic, but there was only one problem: were there enough clients in this very small town to make a riding school economically viable?

The cold caravan also caused me to get very tired and sore in the back. I went to the doctor's and found out I had developed a kidney infection. This caused further expense, as I now had to rent a small, furnished cottage in the town and walk down to the stables every day.

Things just were not going right. I decided to take Monty for a ride out of town, as I felt upset. I called him and he came trotting up as he always did. After putting the bridle on, I vaulted up bareback and rode him straight through the town and out the other side. I wanted to have a good gallop, but could not get off the tar road, as it was fenced both sides, so I just rode on. Soon I came to a river and found a way off the road to the river banks. As the recent rains had made the grass very soggy, it was still not suitable, even for a canter, so I leapt off and found a rock to sit on, while Monty had a munch of the grass.

I watched the swollen river swinging downstream. We cannot see the wind that howls and whistles through the grasses, but oh, can we feel it. It is the same with the Holy Spirit of God: we feel Him – the Lord inside us, the glowing warmth, the power to carry on, to try and serve and love God through our work. Why am I so tired? Because I worry and doubt the future here. If the Lord wants me here, He will not let me starve. If He does not want me here, He will let me know.

I looked back at the swollen river. The waters were not fighting its flow, they flowed with the guidance of the river banks, and they reached their destination, though it was over 500 miles to the sea. I had been resisting God. I had not come to Him for guidance, and I was trying to run my own life instead. Was it too late to change?

'Lord God,' I prayed, 'forgive me. You are my boss and I want to work for You. Will You take over my future? I will do my best. May I leave it to You to take care of my future or is this foolish? If I trust You, then it's not foolish, as who better could handle my future? No one. With Your strength I can do it, but without You I'm nothing, so I will trust in You, all of me. I love You Lord.'

I looked at my watch: 4.00 pm. Time to get back.

I meant that prayer and I knew that God answered prayer. He had answered me and healed Jacky Boy. He had also answered my prayer in the mountains when I became a Christian. I felt so much better. I vaulted up onto Monty and rode slowly back to the stables, deep in thought. I so wanted to succeed here, to have the stables all built up and successful. Then I was going to tell my parents, as I wanted to surprise them. They thought I was still in Drakensberg, and I was keeping this a secret, so that my father would be proud of my success with horses. I did have the excellent results from the one and only horse show we had ridden in here in Barkly East, but that was all.

Then I thought of writing to John to ask if it would be possible to go back to where I was so happy working with the boys. I realized that this was far more important than trying to earn extra money. I felt I had been able to help and encourage the boys as I worked alongside them. I felt I had made a big mistake leaving them. Then I thought, 'Well it's in God's hands now, I'll just wait a while.'

The next morning I had to take Gunflash down to the forge for new shoes. I got up early, did all the mucking out and then saddled Gunflash to get to the forge at 10.00 am. It was not far, just ten minutes away.

The farrier was just finishing the last shoe when there was a knock and surprise of all surprises my parents walked in. I simply burst into tears.

'How did you know I was here?' I exclaimed.

'We didn't,' came the reply.

'Then how did you get here?' I inquired again.

'We don't know.'

'That's crazy, you must know.'

'Well let's start from the beginning,' my mother went on. 'We were on our way to East London for a holiday pulling our new caravan, when Jim suddenly said, "We have to go to Barkly East." I asked him, "Why Barkly East?" and your father replied, "I don't know, we just have to go." Your brother Peter said from the back, "Not that one-horse town.

Nothing happens there." But, by this time, your father was turning the car round towards Barkly East.'

'Well we didn't quite make it to Barkly East last night, so we booked in at the hot springs at Alowal North and had a good swim.'

'Yes,' said Peter, 'and dad got us up first thing this morning to come here and he did not even know why he was coming here. Can you believe that?'

'Yes, well you are here aren't you?' I said. 'But how did you know you were coming for me?' I asked.

'Easy,' replied my father. 'We saw two riders on horseback riding down the main street, and then we knew it was something to do with you. So we asked them, "Is there anyone called Suzanne Ratcliffe here?" "Yes," came the reply, "she's at the forge getting her horse re-shod." So they showed us where to come and here we are.'

'Wow!' I said. 'What time was it when you turned the caravan round to come?' I asked.

'About 4.00 pm,' said my father.

My hair nearly stood up, and I went all tingly all over. That was the precise moment I gave my future to the Lord. The Lord had answered my prayer that fast! He had sent my parents!

'Well how are you?' my father asked.

Slowly it all came out and I told them the whole story.

'Come back to Port Elizabeth,' my father said. 'The Longfield Riding Centre next door to us is up for rent. I will get onto that straight away for you and get down as soon as you can. We have enough stables free for your horses in the meantime.'

'I haven't a heavy-duty licence,' I remarked.

'Well then, get that Mike friend of yours to drive you down. Phone him today.'

My father was always a very strong-willed man. His 'yes' meant yes, and his 'no' a definite no. When he made up his mind about something, nothing could change it. He expected his orders to be obeyed.

I did obey. God had led him there and I believed that God had used my father to bring me into His perfect will. There was no need to think any further, only to follow.

Chapter 11

Longfield

Soon everything was organised. Mike did agree to drive the horses and horsebox to Port Elizabeth and though the Barkly East Council were disappointed, they were at least pleased that it had happened before the building work started.

Mike arrived early the following Saturday morning. We loaded up the horses, I packed up my old grey combi and we were on our way.

With the better roads of the Eastern Cape the journey went quite quickly. We arrived before dark and unloaded the horses.

My father had done a good job with the new lease and we could move into the premises in two weeks time. Meanwhile the grooms would take care of my horses, and as there was not much for me to do, I decided I could run Mike back to Drakensberg and visit the boys at the same time.

Mike stayed with us for the night and the next morning we set off back to Barkly East to collect his car and from there to the school.

We arrived towards evening. John put me up and Mike went down to his accommodation at the school. I could not think how I could have left this beautiful place, and yet it seemed as if I had not left at all, because of the way John and the others treated me.

Next morning I went down to the school early. I knew the boys loved their early morning swim before school, so I went straight to the swimming pool.

'Hey!' shouted Gavin. 'Suzanne's here, race you to her.'

Splashing through the pool, the boys swam and pulled themselves up towards me.

'You've come back to us. Why did you leave us? It's boring without you. Thought you'd come back?'

'Just for a visit,' I replied. 'Anyway how are you?'

'Well, Nicky is OK, but it's just a bit boring without you, that's all.'

'Not completely,' said Gavin. 'Tell her about John's mother.'

'Oh yes, she caught us eating apples from her apple orchard. She knew we did it at night and stayed up to catch us. Well, we had put clothes under our bed blankets and we were coming along the passage way when we heard a noise. "Into the showers," someone whispered, and we all quickly got off the passage way into the showers, straight into John's mother, who had been hiding there to catch us. She let out the most terrible scream, as we did ourselves and we all fled in all directions.'

'We woke up the whole school,' said another. 'John's mother was so confused, that though she caught all of us, she could not see who was who as we all fled.'

'I don't know who got the greater fright, her or us,' said another.

'Hey, there's the bell. Must go, see you later.'

'Hope you come and hear us sing on Wednesday,' said another.

Then they were gone.

Going into breakfast at the school, John called me over to sit with them.

'I have a job for you,' he said. 'That's if you can stay a few days.'

'Yes,' I said.

'The film crew arrives today and I have to be somewhere else. Will you look after them for us? I want you to give them a champagne breakfast tomorrow and then take them riding and flying between their filming sessions with the boys.'

It was good to be so welcomed, and the next morning it was great fun preparing the breakfast on the front lawn, heralded by Champagne Castle itself. The film crew were also a fun group of photographers who definitely preferred flying to riding, so at 11.00 am I took them down to the airfield in my old grey combi. The plane could take up to six people, so that meant I could go up as well.

It was a wonderful flight, soaring between the mountain crags. We saw new valleys and mountain shapes I had never seen before. At one stage the thermals made the plane very bumpy and it was almost scary flying between the mountains so close to the rocks. The photographers also got a number of aerial photos of the school, as we circled down to land.

Soon it was time to return to Port Elizabeth, so after a wonderful few days, I said goodbye to everyone and drove away to my new home.

It was good to have a few days to organise everything before moving into Longfield, and also to have some time to spend with my parents and brothers. The day before the move I went across to the now empty house to work out where to put my things and what I needed to buy.

It was an old house, and the kitchen, especially, was in poor condition with rotting floorboards. The dining room and lounge were nice though, and two of the bedrooms were fine. Like the kitchen, the third bedroom was also suffering from rotten floorboards. Anyway, the house was good enough for me.

The stables were quite nice, built round a courtyard and facing out into a long field. They just needed paint, and a lawn put into their centre.

The next day I moved in and got straight to work. I then brought my horses across and wasted no time in opening Longfield up as a riding school.

During the next three months I managed to get six livery and about 25 to 30 pupils a week. This was already better than at Barkly East, but it did seem I was having problems getting my books to balance. To correct this, I decided to sell Head Hunter. Being a thoroughbred he was the least used, and I managed to get 400 Rand for him which was a great help.

After another month I was again having trouble getting my books to balance. I could not sell more horses or I would not have enough to continue running the riding school.

It was then that I decided to come to the Lord with my problem. I had given my life and my future to the Lord, but I had never thought of giving Him my work as well – the riding school. But to give Him a riding school struggling to survive? Surely not. Yet that is what I did.

I gave the riding school to the Lord in prayer and it appeared that He received it, for He told me, to find stabling elsewhere for one of my livery.

Could I be hearing right? I was trying to get more livery, not giving them away. I prayed again.

I was sure I heard wrongly, but the answer was, 'Is it My school or your school?'

'Your school,' I replied.

Now I had to obey God.

I phoned up an opposition riding school to ask them if they had room for another livery that I wished to send them, and was told they had room.

I then approached the client, who did not have lessons from me, and put the proposition to her as well. Although surprised by my feeble excuse of cutting down on livery, reluctantly she did agree to move her horse.

The horse and client left, but I was still bewildered as to why the Lord should ask me to do such a strange thing. It had certainly been a difficult command for me to obey.

The day after the horse left some new pupils joined us and suddenly we seemed to be out of the red and making a bit of money.

Another month passed. I had to find an auditor to do my books for me. He had a good look through them.

'Look at this,' he said. 'Look at your horse feed prices and compare them with your livery prices. You are under-charging for your livery. You need to put up each livery by

20 Rand immediately, if you are going to cover costs and make some profit from them.'

All of a sudden I realized why the Lord had commanded me to let go of that livery. I never knew the Lord knew anything about finance. I never knew that He accepted us at our word and actually took control of our lives and work. I never knew that He would actually accept my riding school in debt and turn it round to be financially successful.

I thought I knew about horses, but the Lord knows so very much more. 'From now on,' I thought, 'every decision I ever make will be made in prayer.' Only God knows all the pros and cons of every decision. We can only make a decision based on the limited information that we have. We never know all the information and even if we had the intelligence of the finest computer, the computer can only analyse the data put into it. But God knows everything. **It is actually impossible to make a mistake if God has given us the decision while in prayer.**

Chapter 12

Going Deeper

The riding school was now becoming more and more successful. I also started to come to the Lord more often, even over small things. I also began to read the Bible more every day. In every detail the Lord seemed to answer me.

One day I decided I would try to go into a church again. I had not gone to one since the chapel experience, following the beautiful conversion I had had in the mountains. I decided to go to St Johns, a large Anglican church, the very church that had put me off church years before.

I went the next Sunday and sat near the back. The same priest was still there, very tall and thin, and the congregation looked just the same.

Yet there was a difference. As the congregation began to sing, they seemed to sing with all their hearts, the prayers seemed more alive and the people seemed to radiate love, whereas before they had seemed very stiff, correct and cold.

What had happened I did not know, but I certainly intended to find out. After the service we were invited over to the hall for tea and biscuits, which was also new. I then began to speak to different people and they told me how the Holy Spirit was being poured out on their church and was changing them. Well, I could see they had already been changed and they invited me to the Wednesday Midweek Fellowship. I was excited to say yes.

The Midweek Fellowship was even better than the church service. The Lord's presence was there, I could feel it. There was a genuine love for the Lord. It was reality, and it was glorious.

These people had received what I had received up in the mountains. They had come to know God and hear Him in the way I was experiencing alone. Suddenly I was no longer alone in my experience of God. God had met us where we were, whether in a church, or alone on a mountain.

They believed that the healings and miracles recorded in the Acts of the Apostles were for today, not just for the twelve Apostles. They believed the Bible, as I did. I was so overjoyed.

They also said there was even a deeper level than that of salvation and that would be the baptism in the Holy Spirit.

The following week was Pentecost Sunday. I deeply desired to be baptised in the Holy Spirit as well. I got up early next Sunday, and got to church well before time, filled with expectancy. Would God baptise me? The service went on, but nothing happened to me and I went home a bit disappointed.

I searched myself. Maybe I just was not good enough, and maybe next year God would consider me. I would just do my best to become a better person.

On Wednesday I went to the Midweek Fellowship again. Again it was wonderful and I was learning more about God all the time. I also learnt that we can't tell God what to do, but must trust Him to do things in His own timing.

That night when I got home, I gave it some more thought and went to bed. I was just going off to sleep when suddenly I seemed immersed in a beautiful light. God's presence seemed to fill me and fill me and I began to praise Him as never before. Was this the baptism in the Holy Spirit? It was so glorious that it just must be. I also knew that my life had taken on a new dimension, and could never be the same again. I knew that, from that moment, I was a new person in the Lord.

Next Sunday I could hardly wait to tell the Rev. John Silver of my experience. He was standing near another minister at the time and listened to me, then turned to the other minister and said, 'This is for you.'

'Suzanne, meet Brian Bird. He is just planning a new church nearer to you and it's full of new Christians just baptised in the Holy Spirit as you have been. They are also younger people, such as you are.'

From then on I became a member of St Nicholas in Charlo and was to learn much more about God, under the anointed teaching of Brian Bird.

I thought back to the wonderful things that had happened, grabbed some paper and wrote *Silent Watch*.

The icy grip of the world struck into my very bones.
I was alone, afraid of the searching fingers of life's confusion,
Hard and ice clad, I would stare at the wind swept skies.

Something in the sky's timeless glory stood silent watch,
Its perfect loveliness seemed strange and unreal
There was a sacred wonder. Showing through its beauty.

A beauty that awoke my mind, to the way of God,
A love that melted my heart, to read the Bible,
A light that revealed the truth, given by Jesus.

Like a star to guide the way, He led me to the fellowship
of God's people, the Church.

Silently, alone, the skies of all earth's beauty
Showed me this new life, a life in the beauty of God's love.

Chapter 13

The Riding Courses

We were still a young riding school, so I wrote to Vryhiel, Piet Ratief and Sasolburg just outside Johannesburg to see if they would still like me to give riding courses at their riding clubs.

The response was excellent, as all three towns still wanted me to come and all I had to do was give them the dates and they would arrange everything.

I wrote back and soon everything was arranged for the following holidays, when a lot of my own pupils would be away.

At the same time I was also training students to become riding instructors and Penny from Johannesburg was on a course with me. Penny was a responsible girl and able to carry on while I was away.

The first two-day course was in Sasolburg: four lessons and two lectures a day, for two groups of six riders. The course went very well and they made provisional dates for another course during the next holidays.

As I had a three-day break before Vryhied, it gave me a chance to visit the Drakensberg Boys Choir School on the way, so I set off in that direction.

It was a good five-hour drive and about half-way there my old grey combi began to make a terrible noise and ground to a halt. I tried to start it, but the engine would not turn. I got out of the combi not knowing what to do, but seeing a pick-up truck in the distance, I ran across the road to wave it down. It stopped, and I told the driver the problem. He said he would tow me to his garage in Vreda and there they may be able to help me.

Half-an-hour later we reached the garage. They told me that the old combi had seized up and a new engine would cost me 800 Rand, but they could do nothing for a few days. I told them I had to be at another course in three days time, and they showed me a much more modern combi for sale for only 1,200 Rand – it even had a radio. I got into it; I would love to own it, but had no money to buy it. It was out of the question. It was then that another man offered me 400 Rand for my combi as it was. That was a good offer, but 400 Rand could not buy a 1,200 Rand combi.

'Think about it,' he said. 'I'll come back tomorrow.'

All I had on me was 200 Rand from the Saolburg course. Where would I stay?

'Is there a hotel in the village?' I asked.

'No,' said the garage owner, 'but I have some Christian friends who will put you up for the night.'

After 5.00 pm he took me round to introduce me to his friends. They were lovely Christians and welcomed me into their home, gave me a lovely supper and showed me to their small and comfortable guest room.

I was extremely grateful to them and left the next morning as they left to go to work. I went straight to the garage where the owner seemed to be waiting for me.

'Sell your combi to this man,' he said, 'and put the 400 Rand down on that newer combi. I'll have it ready for you at 10.00 am.'

'But what about the rest?' I said.

'Pay me the rest when you get home. Here's my address.'

I could not believe my ears. That garage man trusted me. What else could I do, but to do as he said?

By 10.00 am I was on my way in my newer grey combi with the radio on. 'The Lord must have spoken to that garage man,' I thought, 'for him to trust me so.' I also found out that Vreda is Afrikaans for peace. What a beautiful peaceful village Vreda was as well.

It was lunchtime when I reached the school.

'Just in time for lunch,' said John's mother. 'Well, don't stand there, come in and sit down and don't eat all the potatoes.'

'Thank you,' I replied, sitting down opposite her.

'The boys break up for their July holidays in two days time. Could you do the religious studies with them?' she went on. 'The teachers need more time to mark their papers.'

'With pleasure,' I replied.

'You'll have to stay in a staff bedroom upstairs this time,' she said. 'How long are you here for?'

'Two nights,' I replied.

'That will do just nicely,' she said.

It was good to see the boys again. Nicky was doing a good job with them and I joined in on a hack with them that afternoon.

The next morning I had a nice little talk prepared, bringing in Christmas, Good Friday and Easter to cover the gospel in today's situation.

I worked through the classes starting with the younger ones and finishing with the more senior classes. I had some good responses from the children and prayed with them to receive the Lord into their hearts.

Standards 6 and 7 were put together into one class for religious studies and I gave them the same talk, but with a bit more detail. I then challenged them as to who would like to receive the Lord into their hearts and every hand went up.

I started to pray and suddenly every boy began to cry. I stared in amazement. The power of God had come upon every boy.

One shouted out, 'My ankle has just been healed.'

'I am healed as well,' came another voice.

'Jesus is real,' said another.

'Come into my heart,' said another.

'Thank you Jesus . . . Praise you . . . Forgive me.'

They were crying with repentance and joy at the same time and were also getting quite excited. I led them through the repentance prayer and then we all thanked the Lord together. These boys were not at all shy and the Lord had truly touched them.

We spent the entire afternoon together. The boys had loads of questions, which I answered as best I could.

'Please come and hear us sing tonight.'

I said I would.

'We are going to sing for the soldiers on the border next week and the next. This is our last practice.'

That night the boys sang like angels, so much so that their conductor said, 'I've never heard you sing so well, what's got into you?'

'It's Jesus,' they all shouted out in one accord.

He looked a bit amazed.

The next morning I was on my way again to Vryhied. I loved teaching there and some of the children had managed to buy better horses. Mrs Mossip also encouraged me to share my faith with them, as she and Enid were already Christians. The course went well.

Next onto Piet Ratief. Here I stayed with a German family. They showed me into an old-fashioned room with a lit candle on the dressing table, and a bed that sank down so deeply it was hard to get out of again. The candle flickered and glowed up warm.

The Candle

The candle flickers and glows upwards
It gives off light and warmth,
It guides the way, if held, through the dark,
It is placed on an old table in front on a mirror
And the reflection gives an even greater light.

A candle is a symbol of ancient times
As it gives of itself in a loving peaceful way,
We can imagine the lit wick, along with the wax
Quietly creating the flame of energy
That lights the way or guides my pen.

In the Bible a flame is linked with the Holy Spirit,
A glow in our hearts that lights the truth,
Shows us the way through the world
And gives us the power to obey
What the Lord gives us to do.

When we give of ourselves and obey God
Or share His word in a loving way,
It gives us an even greater light and power
To complete what the Lord has given us to do.

It is when we received the gift of the Holy Spirit
That the Lord lights us with His Holy flame,
As we have to light a candle.
For as a candle is made to be lit with light
So we are created to know our God.

Lord, I am simple like a candle
Allow me to give to others, what a candle gives
If a candle with Your help, Lord, can teach me this,
Then Lord, light my heart too,
So that we may also teach others this.

Next morning I started with the course at the local polo club, whom I also invited to join the course.

'What do polo riders need lessons for?' they asked.

'To learn to ride with your weight aids, rather than on the horse's mouth,' I replied.

'But we all have Pelhams,' they said.

'That's the problem,' I replied. 'Give me a horse with just a halter on and I will show you.'

They brought me a horse with a halter and saddle and I mounted up to demonstrate the weight aids. It worked and a few extra riders joined the course. We had a lot of fun learning the new techniques, as well as improving the comfort of their horses.

That evening I also went out on a Safari ride on their farm and saw many beautiful wild animals.

The next day was Sunday and we all went to church together, before starting the course. That afternoon I was approached about a horse with a pastern that had been broken for two weeks. They refused to put the polo mare down, as she was their best mare and wanted to breed from her. I said I would come the next morning, before setting off for Johannesburg to watch some international show jumping.

The course ended well and the next morning I went to see the mare. The pastern bone was broken right through and the mare was standing on her fetlock joint. I asked if I could phone Onderstepoort. The vet there said a watermelon bandage was the only hope, but they had left it too long. We went off and bought ten rolls of cotton wool and ten crepe bandages.

I knelt down beside the horse, knowing nothing about setting broken bones, and prayed. The people stared at me in disbelief.

'You can't pray for a horse!' they exclaimed.

I asked them, 'Well, do you want the horse to get well?'

'Yes.'

'Well, please let me do it in the only way I know.'

I prayed for the horse, lifted the leg, tried to line up the broken pastern bone as best I could with my fingers and wrapped the cotton wool and bandages round it fairly tightly – hopefully tightly enough to keep it firm, but without cutting off the blood supply.

'Leave this on for up to six weeks,' I said. 'Hopefully it may heal enough to breed from her.'

Soon I was back in my treasured combi driving towards Johannesburg – radio on, of course.

I had just driven around the top part of Basuto Land when I felt the Lord say to me, 'Go home.'

'But I wanted to watch the show jumping.'

'Go home.'

I reluctantly turned left towards home, instead of right at the next junction.

'Why home?' I thought. There were only four days left of the holidays. How could I arrange a riding course tonight for tomorrow? But I also had this combi to pay off and not enough money to do so. I figured that if the Lord said, 'Go home,' it must be to run a riding course, instead of watching show jumping.

I made it home by 6.00 pm. I got straight on the phone and within thirty minutes had eight riders who were happy to come on a four-day course starting tomorrow, Tuesday 10.00 am, and ending Friday 4.00 pm.

Penny had done a good job while I was away and was an enormous help with the following four-day riding course.

The following week I was able to send a cheque to Vreda garage for the full amount owing on the combi. God is so very, very good.

Two weeks later I had a phone call from the Drakensberg Boys Choir School. The boys had sung exceptionally well to the soldiers on the border and had even led some of them to the Lord. Praise God.

Sometime later I also had a letter from the owners of the polo horse that I had prayed for. She was completely healed and sound.

The following year when I visited them again she had had a beautiful foal and was back on the polo field. The healed pastern was able to stand up to the heavy demands of polo playing. Only God could do that.

Chapter 14

The Rally

The riding school was growing all the time. We needed to build a brick labourer's cottage for our new groom and sort out the normal ups and downs of running a riding school.

One sad thing was that I had caught my star student, Penny, taking the drug dagga. I punished her by banning her from Longfield for two weeks. This upset her and she phoned her Dad, which upset him. He phoned me and shouted at me down the phone.

After a few minutes of this he said, 'Why aren't you shouting back?'

'I am praying for you,' I answered.

'I also believe in God. Do forgive me for shouting at you. You punish my daughter as you think fit. I am sure she will learn from it.'

Whew! I said goodbye, and replaced the receiver.

'Thank you, Lord. You have helped me again.'

I missed Penny during the next two weeks and was pleased to have her back again. She was always a cheerful girl and I believed that she would never touch drugs again. I also began to witness to her about Jesus, and sometimes would stay up late trying to answer her questions.

Church had by now become a regular habit for me and I loved St Nicholas. I was learning much more about Jesus and wanted to do more for Him after the exciting trip doing the courses.

I prayed about this and realized I had plenty of land that I could use for the Lord. It appeared that the Lord wanted me to run some sort of outdoor rally/picnic. I shared this with Brian Bird, 'Youth for Christ' with whom I was also getting more involved, and the minister of the Presbyterian Church where two of my pupils worshipped.

The first thing we did was to set up an inter-denominational weekly prayer meeting for the rally. The Lord gave me 16th December as the date. This caused some concern amongst the church as it was the day when whites won against blacks at what is now called 'blood river', but I refused to change the date.

The Lord met with us at those prayer meetings. Out of them the finer details were arranged: different speakers were invited for ten-minute slots, Youth for Christ said they would do the music and the black township was invited.

At the prayer meeting on 12th November 1979 the following prophecy was given:

> '*"If any man thirst let him come to Me and drink. If any man believes in Me, as the scripture has said, out of his heart shall flow rivers of living water"* (John 7:37).
>
> The mighty hand of God is upon us; He has anointed us to bring good tidings to the poor, to set the oppressed free, to heal the sick and to set His people free.'

The prophecy went on:

> 'We must trust Him, for His ways are not our ways. We must not hinder His Spirit. What has been started in the Spirit must continue in the Spirit, and then God will pour out His living waters – His Holy Spirit will come down upon the gathering. Miracles will happen and people shall be set free from the enemy, physically and spiritually, from bondage and disease.'

The presence of God was so strong upon us all. The Lord had truly spoken to us, and we would never forget that wonderful prayer meeting. Why had God chosen 16th December? Well, we had to trust Him, that was all.

During the next four weeks all the final arrangements were made. We also white-washed the stables, painted the doors black, mowed the field and made everything as attractive as we could.

Our new groom was white-washing the stables. As I watched him brushing the strokes of white-wash on the walls, I suddenly visualised Jesus in him. I became both slightly shocked and much humbled as I realised, 'Jesus is in me ... Jesus is in him ... Jesus is on the side of the poor ... I am rich in comparison – rich enough to make me change my ways more and to treat all people as I would treat Jesus. If Jesus created every good work, then every good work is God's creation shining through ... shining through our black grooms ... Jesus shining through him, God bless him.'

I prayed, 'Lord, help me to praise and encourage my workers more and do all I can to keep them happy, for Your sake, Amen.'

Soon it was 16th December. The black people arrived first, by the busload. More and more buses came – there were people everywhere. Then some whites also began to arrive and Youth for Christ started with some music and singing.

The Lord had given me Psalm 107 to read. I was nervous, as I had never read in public before, and I had prayed a lot to make sure I was within the Lord's anointing. I needed His help very badly to read this.

'Oh give thanks to the Lord for He is good,' I began. I read the first verses and then stopped.

'Have any of you been to prison or lost in the desert and He has set you free?'

A few hands went up. I read on about the sick being healed and stopped again.

'Have any of you been sick and the Lord has healed you?'

More hands went up. I carried on:

'Lost, far from shore and the Lord has led you to shore?'

A couple of hands went up.

'Lost in utter darkness and the Lord has bought you into His wonderful light?'

Many hands went up. I came to the last verse of the psalm and read:

'Whoever is wise let him give heed to these things; let men consider the steadfast love of the Lord.'

Looking across the crowd, I said, 'This psalm was written in the time of David, many years before Jesus was born, yet some here today have been touched by this psalm in healing, deliverance and new life. Put up your hands again, if you have been touched in these ways.'

Many hands were going up amongst the crowd.

'Everyone look! Look at the hands! But maybe,' I went on, 'there are people here who have never yet been touched by God, who are still living in darkness, or are sick and have not yet been healed by God, who have problems and have not yet been delivered by God. If there is anyone like that who would like the touch of God on your lives today, come forward now.'

Many people began to come forward. Now what?

'Help me Lord.' I prayed, 'I can't pray for all these people.'

'Call for counsellors in the crowd' came a small voice.

'Any counsellors, please come forward to help me pray for all these people.'

Some counsellors came forward and we divided the group into three.

'Those to receive the Lord in their hearts over here. Those needing healing over there. Those needing deliverance or with other problems this way.'

Soon there were counsellors dealing with each group and the next speaker took the mike to carry on with the rest of the crowd.

'The counsellors left over, come with me into the old horse box to pray.'

It was actually quite hard to pray, because of the shrieks and noises coming from where the counsellors were ministering to the sick and the oppressed.

We stepped out of the horsebox, to find a lady on the ground.

'Is she OK?' I asked the counsellor.

'Don't worry,' he said, 'the Lord has slain her in the Spirit and is healing her.'

I had never seen anything like that before, but sure enough, after another ten minutes, the lady stood up and began to leap around and praise the Lord for healing her. Others also began to dance with joy, and raising their hands high above their heads, began to thank God for their healings. It was so wonderful to watch.

I suddenly realised that God's mighty hand was moving.

'He is here', I shouted. 'Praise our living God, bless His holy name. To God, all things are possible.'

Now I was seeing His hand at work: how He was strengthening our faith. For God is a God of miracles, a God who loves to heal His people, to set them free, to loose those in bondage and bring them into His glorious light. I was seeing His prophecy to us come true right in front of my eyes.

That was not all that was to happen that day. A further twenty-two came forward at the end of Brian Bird's talk, to give their lives to the Lord in full-time service.

At another time a different preacher read from Scripture about the Lord's triumphant entry into Jerusalem and people complaining about the noise. Some of the Pharisees in the multitude said to Him *'Teacher, rebuke Your disciples.'* He answered, *'I tell you, if these were silent, the very stones would cry out'* (Luke 19:39–40).

At that moment every horse in the stables turned their heads towards us and neighed. There was a holy silence amongst us, as if God's presence hovered over us. The words of Jesus seemed to say the same to us today, as well.

Suddenly we all took each other's hands and began to dance around the whole field praising God – all 400 of us, black and white together. Tears were flowing from our eyes in the wonderful presence of God. A black lady with a strong voice then led us in song: 'Bind us together Lord, bind us together in love', and the musicians joined in. It was glorious – so spontaneous – and as the dance round the field came to an end, we began to hug each other. Blacks and whites hugging each other? It was then, that a black man went up to the mike and took it.

He said, 'Today 16th December, the whites fought us at the blood river and won. But today a greater thing is happening. Today 16th December, blacks and whites are standing together in victory; victory over the forces of evil.'

What a wonderful end to the most wonderful day. Soon the buses were getting ready to leave and I said goodbye to our new-found friends.

I then simply bowed to God in awe and gratitude for this wonderful day. A day of answered prayer. A day blessed by His Holy presence. A day controlled by His Holy Spirit. A day where God allowed His Holy Spirit to move through His people as rivers of living water to a thirsty people, healing them physically and mentally, truly setting them free, and accepting them as His children. A day where each of the 400 people must surely have known that God is real and true, as more than 60 experienced the great hand of God in a very personal way, and many others testified to His mighty power. I also now knew why God had chosen December 16th for this rally. It was wonderful.

I reflected, 'Praise God for allowing His prophecy over us to come true. Praise God for the miracles and blessings He poured upon His people this day. Praise God for the reconciliation He brought to the 400 of us here today. Praise God for the wonderful response of over 60 people who were touched, healed, set free and reborn into the Kingdom of God.'

The feedback was also encouraging. The whites even enjoyed it so much that they wanted another one.

Then the Rev. Johnson phoned from New Brighton. 'The people are still so happy they have told the whole of New Brighton about it. They say the rally has done a new thing for them in their hearts and this has made them very happy.'

Individuals also phoned up during the week to let us know what God had done for them and all had truly been set free.

Mandy phoned and said she had been delivered and set free from epilepsy. She had suffered at least two fits a day

Longfield – The Horsebox church which became too small for the 'Kragga Kamma Church'. It is still a church today.

since birth, but now she was 100% healed and rejoicing in the Lord.

Youth for Christ took on the follow-up for all the new conversions and Brian Bird, along with the Rev. Johnson, organized a leadership course for those wanting to serve the Lord full-time.

Out of this rally the Rev. Johnson and I found ourselves starting up a black church in the garden, and converted the black horsebox into a chapel.

Christmas was upon us. It was Christmas Eve, and Rev. Johnson was led by God to come to the local *shabeen* – the place where the blacks came to buy drink with their Christmas bonuses. But now the 'Man of God' was there, they could not buy drink until the 'Man of God' left and the *shabeen* got fuller and fuller. Rev. Johnson began to preach and God poured out His Spirit on every person. All accepted the Lord into their hearts, including the owner of the *shabeen*.

They then began to praise God and this carried on the whole night. At 6.00 am I could hear the people walking home praising God. There were no drunken people in our area that Christmas Day. The blacks said 'We don't need the sprit of alcohol anymore for we now have Spirit of Jesus in our hearts and that is much, much better.'

Soon our church became far too big for our garden. We showed them the film *Jesus of Nazareth* and a kindly farmer offered us his large barn for the church. We moved there, as the church had already grown to 400 plus each Sunday.

Chapter 15

Learning from Simple Things

I was spending time with God . . .

All is quiet, all is at peace. The trees stand tall, their branches uplifted to the skies.

The smell of fresh leaves tint the air, and petals glisten on still waters. I look; I wonder; I learn. How great is God's great love.

Something emerges from the stillness, no more solid than the distant chatter of birds, yet something with so much meaning.

The silent voice becomes clearer and gently the reflection of God's beauty whispers a message in my heart: 'Be still and know that I am God. Let My beauty reflect through your life. Allow your tense muscles to spill into quietness. Yield to the guidance of My Holy Spirit as the trees yield to the breeze. Yield your mind into My guidance and move forward boldly, and as you learn to give freely of yourself for others, so My light shall shine forth through you in a quiet glowing beauty.'

There had been so much excitement with the rally, yet there was something even more important for me to learn: to spend more time with God, to learn from Him, to grow in Him, to enjoy His presence.

Only out of our time spent in God's presence is there any chance of hearing Him speak to us, and obeying Him.

As I sought to seek His presence more, I began to notice and learn even more.

I had been overdoing it again as it had been busy. Life was just moving too fast and time spent with God always seems to be the first thing to suffer.

Yet I knew that there is nothing more beautiful than the wonder of God's presence; nothing more perfect than waiting on Him.

...I see ice caps upon a tall mountain. It's a beautiful ice-covered peak reaching up into the sky. Only one problem – only mountaineers can reach it...

I see many of us as ice caps. We have received the living waters; we have had a mountain-top experience with God. We have received the gifts of the Holy Spirit. The problem is that, spiritually, we are so high in the clouds, we have not yet come down to earth.

God does not give the mountain's rain to stay up there as snow. He sends the heat of the sun to melt the ice, so that it may flow down the mountain slopes to bring life to the valleys below.

Neither does God give us His Holy Spirit to lie frozen in our hearts, but to flow out to all we meet, as rivers of living water, that bring life to all.

Only after people have been blessed by God's living waters can their roots begin to go deep into the Word of God. It is only as this strengthens the stems by prayer and action that people can truly grow up into the love of God's presence, receive more of the Holy Spirit and yield much fruit for God.

My thoughts turn to a simple school pony. How many hours a year does one pony spend teaching children to ride: 600 to 1,000 hours a year?

Just one pony takes that time in his work to yield to the control of every individual rider who cares to sit on his back. It's quite fantastic.

We do not train a pony and let him stand dormant. We expect him to yield himself to us in work, in whatever work we ask of him, and the pony does it without question.

Let us turn our hearts to God. Let us yield our hearts to Him, to melt before His presence, and walk forth into this world.

Let us turn to God in prayer, be obedient in our actions, then live to His glory in love for all mankind.

Suddenly we will see results, but not of ourselves; we shall see God's glory flow, even out of us.

We then become pure and clean, filled with grace and love, and like channels of blessing to everyone we meet.

It's then we look to Jesus, filled with gratitude and awe, for rivers of living water can flow even through us. All this can be achieved, without tension or stress, by simply being yielded to Him.

I was learning to hear God through everything; even a flower could speak to me.

A flower struggles beneath the hard, crusted earth until, somehow, it makes a breakthrough into the strange new world above. It appears and faces towards the sunlight, getting its first feel of the gusty winds.

The flower is committed to a brand new world, whatever it may hold, drawing up the sap through its roots and reaching up ahead into the great unknown.

Yielded to the grace of God and the elements of nature, the flower soon gives itself to this world of ours, allowing nature to enable its petals to unfold into the vulnerable beauty of its tender heart.

The flower has a mission ahead: it is to cheer a human in hospital, a mother, a loved one, a funeral, a birth, a garden, a home, a small child, or to die and reproduce. Whatever the future, it yields fully, to bless, to brighten, and to cheer.

Is not a flower a symbol of love; something of beauty, colour and scents; something to cheer, bring joy and love? Everywhere it brightens its surroundings, shining forth its reflection of loveliness.

The darker the room, the greater its attraction, drawing humans to the beauty of life. Whatever its task, the flower is there, fully committed to its task on earth.

And us? Can we yield to our Creator as a flower does? Can we take the steps to follow in the steps of Jesus? Can we yield to Him fully, for Him to change us into our full potential, allowing Him to open us up for His love to shine through?

Are we fully committed to our mission on earth? Are we dedicated to give our best, whatever the call? Do we have love like that of a flower, content to give, even in adverse conditions?

I bow before God, yielded and still as a waiting bud; can I take that step like a simple flower? A promise too great to behold – God wants me as His flower to yield the beauty of His love to a dry and thirsty land.

'Me? Not me, my Lord,' I may say. 'I'm not worthy.'

But did not God use even a little flower?

'Then, Lord, use me. Make me, Lord, as a total flower, a flower for You.'

But God needs many flowers of every type and description to fulfil His will on earth, and to shine the truth of His Kingdom through to the world. He does not want just to export flowers as missionaries, but wants flowers that bring beauty right where we are, in our own backyards and gardens. And that is you and me, right here where we are now, shining as lights for Jesus. Each unique person with his own special gifts has his own special work to do for the glory of God, for as Psalm 103:15–18 says:

As for us, our life is like grass
We grow and flourish like a wild flower
Then the wind blows on it and it is gone
No one sees it again.
But for those who honour the Lord
His love lasts forever
And his goodness endures for all generations
Of those who are true to His covenant
And who faithfully obeys His commands.

It was a few days later that my mother phoned me from Kragga Kama Riding School next door.

'Suzanne, Bonny is sick, he cannot breath properly. A little girl of friends of ours hired him out for an hour yesterday. She is supposed to be a good rider, but I'm afraid she galloped him and now he can hardly breath. I'll send Bonny over with our groom for you to look at him.'

'Fine,' I said. 'Send him over now.'

In fifteen minutes Bonny and his groom 'Banana' arrived. His head hung low and his sides were heaving. Old and weary, the pony staggered towards me, lifted his heavy head and rested it on my arms. Bonny had given all he had to give; he had no more to give, except to put his head into my arms. He looked at me, his soft brown eyes watering and aged.

I realised his wind was broken and his end was near. Bonny had taught thousands of children how to ride and had given his best, serving humans all his life. What could I do for him, apart from retire him?

'Bonny,' I whispered, with tears, 'if I could give as you have given, with the love that you have, with your unselfishness and honesty, I still could not match up to your beauty. As poor and ugly as you may look, I know you are a wonderful pony. May God bless you, Bonny, with all the contentment that you deserve.'

My thoughts went back to the first time I had seen Bonny years before. I had gone out to Green Bushes to buy a cob gelding called Tally, and this pony had come limping up, put his big head in my arms, just where it was now, and looked up at me in way as if to say, 'Please buy me.'

'How much do you want for this one?' I called out.

'Oh Poon, twenty rand will do, for that.'

'OK,' I said. 'I'll buy this one too.'

Bonny had bony lumps on his legs and a bigger one on the side of his face due to lack of calcium. He also had what looked like deformed hoofs and was still a stallion. He was also rather thin and ribby at the time.

Once I got Poon home, I renamed him Bonny. I soon got the farrier out to deal with his deformed hoofs and put shoes on, then a vet came to geld him, de-worm him and file his teeth. He soon put on weight and became one of my best school ponies for children.

Now Bonny was much older, somewhere in his twenties, and with incurable broken wind as well.

'Lord,' I prayed, 'this pony does not deserve an end like this. Only you can heal him, if that be Your will. And Lord, help me to become to You as this pony has been to me. Thank you Lord, Amen.'

I let go of Bonny's head and gave him a pat.

'You can take him back now Banana, please.'

'Ya, Miss,' he replied, and taking Bonny by his halter led him back next door shaking his head.

'Banana must think I am crazy,' I thought as I went inside, 'talking to ponies and praying. Oh well, who cares.'

The next morning my mother phoned again.

'Suzanne,' she said, 'Bonny is better.'

'He can't be,' I answered, 'broken wind is incurable.'

'He is better,' she insisted. 'I don't know what you did to him, but whatever you did, it worked.'

I suddenly remembered, 'Oh yes, I prayed.'

But surely not . . . and so fast! I felt humbled.

'Mom,' I said, 'can we retire Bonny to Riding for the Disabled, so no child can ever mistreat him again?'

'What an excellent idea,' she replied. 'You make the arrangements and he can go to them.'

Riding for the Disabled were thrilled to receive Bonny, and he went on to teach disabled children to ride for the further seven years of his life.

As a result of what happened to Bonny neither my parents nor I ever hired out a horse or pony again, unless supervised.

Chapter 16

Whipalong Stud

The phone rang. It was an invitation to teach a course at Whipalong Stud in the Karoo. The problem for me was that they wanted me to teach 'Saddle Seat Equitation' for riding American Saddle bred horses. I did not know very much about this riding style, so I asked them to give me some time to think about it before making a decision.

I then saddled up and took out five children for a ride through the woods at the back of the riding school.

Jacky Boy pranced ahead, ears pricked, his big head lifted and trotting on eagerly. It was good to be out and he was soon cantering on under his rider, without a thought about the miracle of his leg holding up.

Little did his rider know of Jacky's past.

Yet Jacky Boy moved on. God had healed him and that was enough. He was able to walk, trot, gallop and jump. Surely that was enough.

By faith the impossible had come to pass. Jacky Boy could walk, trot and canter, and now he was helping me to make a decision. How many of us can walk by faith, keeping our eyes on Christ? How many of us can move ahead, leaving past doubts behind? How many of us can serve the Lord, believing He can do all things?

The Scriptures are alive. Behind every word of God is the power of heaven. To walk by faith for Jesus is victory, for *'I can do all things through Christ who strengthens me,'* and *'it's not by might nor by power, but by My Spirit says the Lord of Hosts.'*

During the storm on the lake, Jesus said, *'Why are you afraid O men of little faith?'* then *'He rose and rebuked the wind and the sea and there was a great calm'* (Matthew 8:26). Does Jesus have to say the same to us?

So the decision was made. I accepted the invitation and bought a book on 'Saddle Seat Equitation'. Reading this book, I discovered there was very little difference from the dressage seat, or the movements performed, and that my dressage background would actually be a huge asset in the teaching of Saddle Seat equitation.

The phone call had come as a result of a mission our church had given in their area. It had been very successful and I had been introduced to Kate during that weekend. Now Kate had contacted me.

The day approached fast, and soon I was in my grey combi travelling over the mountain range that separated the green coastline from the dryness of the Karoo.

It was about a four-hour drive in the July heat of summer 1980. The hot breeze blew some tumbleweed across the road in front of me in this great dusty expanse of South Africa.

Yet something precious, something so timeless, penetrates your entire being along with the endless beauty of flat-topped hills and the silence of the heralding skies.

Yet silence speaks forth louder than words; the voice of God in all His creation.

Yellow and sunburnt, the grasses rustle their praise to God.

An hour or so later I arrived at the dusty little town near Whipalong Stud. I stopped for some petrol and went into the General Stores for a cool drink and something to eat.

'Are you a stranger here?' remarked the shop keeper.

'Yes,' I replied. 'I'm on my way to Whipalong Stud.'

'You are, are you? We have some groceries to send up to them. Won't you be a sweetie and take them along with you?'

'With pleasure,' I replied.

Back in the combi, with two large boxes of groceries, I finally found the long driveway up to their stud. They lived half-an-hour from the country town.

It was good to see Kate again. She was as friendly as ever with her enormous smile.

'We have twenty riders on the course. I would like you to concentrate on the Equitation classes and I will do the rest.'

Her indoor stables were most impressive with an indoor trotting area at the back about 5 metres wide and at least 40 metres long.

All afternoon riders and their horses were arriving, so we did our best to settle them in. We then had a good Karoo dinner of Karoo beef and vegetables and went to bed.

The next morning was busy separating the riders into four groups of five and getting on with the lessons. That meant eight lessons a day, as each rode twice a day, so it was rather busy.

It was the third day of camp that things began to happen. The hot Karoo sun made riding hard work, and even the horses were not responding well.

'OK, line up and rest,' I commanded.

Suddenly a loose horse trotted past with beauty and grace of movement – head arched, tail high.

'How is it,' asked one of the campers, 'that a loose horse looks so beautiful, but when we get on him, he will move like a donkey?'

'Good question,' I replied. 'Why do you think the loose horse looks so beautiful?'

'He is happy,' said someone.

'And free,' answered another.

'Then why,' I asked, 'don't they feel the same when a person gets on them?'

There was silence. I tried again.

'How do you feel then?'

'Cross,' said someone.

'Why?' I asked.

'Jane took all the bacon at breakfast, so I had none.'

'Oh, jealousy,' I replied.

'Well,' said Jane, 'there were only three bits left anyway.'

'Oh, greed,' I replied. 'And you?' I went on, pointing at a sad-looking rider.

'I had an argument with a friend last night.'

'Oh dear,' I replied. 'So if you are full of these unhappy feelings, how do you expect your horse to be happy when you get on?'

Another silence.

'Maybe we should get rid of these unhappy feelings then?' I suggested.

'How?' asked one of them.

I thought. 'Well the only way I know, is to confess them to Jesus, ask Him to forgive us, and ask Him to fill us with the joy of His presence.'

At that, a tall 19-year-old dismounted, knelt in the dust and said, 'Will you pray for me?'

I had never done that in a riding lesson before, but I went ahead anyway and prayed. After the prayer with everyone watching, he got up smiling and remounted his horse.

'Trot a circle,' I suggested, 'and then canter one.'

He went ahead, his horse moved with a new vigour and the rider's smile became broader and broader as his horse moved better for him than ever before.

All the riders looked on with mouths gaping. 'It worked! Prayer really worked!'

Next day, Sunday, we invited the campers to come to church with us and a few of them did. Guy gave an excellent sermon on the Holy Spirit and was entirely led by the Holy Sprit. As a result three of the campers came forward and were baptised in the Holy Spirit.

Now there were four Christians and they shared what had happened with everyone. Monday was an exciting day. A wild horse was bolting all over the place, and the owner asked me to pray with her for the horse. I did and the horse calmed down immediately. A nervous horse in the stable would not let anyone touch his tail, so his handler asked Guy to pray with him. Immediately the horse calmed down and they could put on the tail set.

In a lesson one girl struggled to achieve a movement with her horse. Hester mounted full of self-confidence and pride and could not do it either and she could ride. She dismounted, very ashamed and red, and then prayed. When she remounted the horse went extremely well and completed the movement easily.

God used the scripture in Zechariah 9:9 to show that pride was not the way, but that Jesus rode with victory, humility and triumph.

That evening the campers who had missed church and what had happened the day before wanted to know what had gone on, so Hester invited them up to her cottage that evening to find out.

Seven campers and Kate came up. Guy spoke to them for a while and the Holy Spirit moved upon us and a further four campers received Christ into their hearts; seven in all. What a wonderful evening.

At about 10.00 pm we drove down to the farm, with the campers singing 'God is so good', all out of tune, while getting out of the car. Hearing their singing, Mac peeped out of the window and saw them hugging each other.

On Tuesday there were more testimonies of God's power: Noreen's answer to yesterday's prayers; new ability to ride, when yielded to God; more positive attitude to the Lord etc.

That night the whole camp came up to the cottage for fellowship. The three big boys accepted the Lord into their hearts and were also baptised in the Holy Spirit.

Every person so far made a very sincere commitment. God's Holy Spirit had touched them in a very special way and almost all of them cried as they as they experienced the Lord.

Kate gave them each a Bible and they kept getting so excited over certain verses, which they shared with each other. What joy this is.

On Wednesday another boy was baptised in the Holy Spirit. During supper I had suggested that we used a shed nearer the farm rather than driving up to Hester's house.

'And what's wrong with my lounge?' said Mac, who was not yet a Christian.

From then on his lounge became our meeting room and Mac made a commitment to the Lord also.

Mac's conversion was a wonderful one, for he was known to be a very tough Karoo farmer. Now he stood up for the Lord, as only Mac could do. He took charge of who would say the grace at meal times.

'Suzanne, fire up a few words for us. Oh, and afterwards pass the cattle fat [that's butter].'

During the next three days the entire camp became Christians and it was then time to go home as the course was successfully completed.

Three weeks later three of the rides entered the South African Championships and managed to come first, second and third.

'Never,' said the judge 'have we had three horses from the same yard placed in this event.'

'It's Jesus,' came the answer.

After the event they were able to lead the judge to the Lord as well, and so in this way the Lord's work was to spread throughout the 'Saddle Seat' horse world.

Chapter 17

Israel

On the drive back from Whipalong Stud my thoughts went back to last March, when I had turned down a trip to Israel.

I had had the money to go, but had felt that the Lord wanted me to give this money to some refugees that the YWAM ship was involved in helping. I am also very ashamed to admit that it took me a full three weeks to obey God and to send them the cheque.

Once I obeyed God, feeling that helping hungry refugees was more important than a holiday, it then took me a further three weeks to get over the disappointment of not going to Israel.

Instead Easter was spent going on a mission to East London with Youth for Christ, which was not easy. We had to sleep on a garage floor with young people of different race groups and this took me a bit of getting used to.

'Yield to those around you' is a hard word. It's not just yielding to God, but to those around you; giving yourself to them, being one of them, letting them throw your pillow, sit on your belongings, play your guitar. But more even than that – to love them. I woke up and thought, 'I could be in Israel and I've given it up to sleep in a garage with teenagers!'

I grabbed my Bible and opened it at random at Ezekiel 34: *'Should not the shepherds feed my sheep ... The weak need strengthening, and the sick need healing, the crippled need binding up, the strayed need to be brought back, the lost need to be sought or they shall become food for all the wild beasts.'*

'Lord,' I prayed, 'if it is Your will I missed the Israel trip to serve You here in East London, then I just praise You, though I feel like crying. Sometimes it is hard to sacrifice, but I do love You and prefer to be in Your will in all things.'

It was only then that I was able to give the Lord my disappointment and get on with my call there, to share the word every night that week at the rallies and coffee bars.

I cannot say what the results were. I did not see many, but the Lord knows.

'At least the Whipalong Stud course made up for it,' I thought. 'There I certainly did see results for the Lord.'

It was dark by the time I got home, but I still had a peep at all the horses and knocked on the door for Penny to let me in. She was also a Christian now.

It was a few days later. The phone rang. It was Faans Klopper from The Christian Embassy.

'Would you be interested in joining us on a trip to Israel and this year's Feast of Tabernacles?'

'I have no money to go,' I replied.

Suddenly I felt the Lord's Holy Spirit come upon me to say yes!

'Well, put my name down anyway,' I said, a little surprised at myself.

The following week I had a phone call inviting me to give a course up in Natal. Then another call, the following day, from a girl at university in Grahamstown who had heard I was going to Natal, asking if I could give five of them a lift to Natal and they would pay me for the petrol.

So the course was arranged. It was a great success and provided just enough to pay for the deposit for the trip to Israel. Now only 1,224.00 Rand to raise – that's a fortune!

The next two weeks went by with no way of raising that amount of money and we only had a few days left before the flight.

It was exactly four days before I was due to leave that a letter arrived in the post with a cheque for exactly 1,224.00 Rand. It was an insurance claim for a sulki cart I had lent to the Port Elizabeth University rag, that had been involved in an accident and squashed flat. The University said they would claim on insurance for it a year ago, but since the cart had only cost me 25 Rand anyway, I had forgotten about it.

I immediately phoned the insurance company who had sent me the cheque.

'The cheque was too much,' I said.

'I would accept it if I were you,' they replied. 'That was the cheapest sulki cart that we could price.'

'Well, thank you very much,' I replied, put down the phone and did a dance round the room. This had to be God supplying the money for Israel and I immediately made arrangements to pay for the trip.

There were only four days to arrange everything. Mike offered to run the stables for four months for me, feed supplies for the horses had to be arranged, bills had to be paid, there was packing to do ... but somehow I did it.

I caught the flight to Johannesburg, met up with people from Harvest Christian Fellowship, and we were on our way.

After a good flight through the night, we stopped in Portugal and then landed at Tel Aviv. From there we caught a bus to Jerusalem. Here we were allocated our rooms and I was put in a room with a lovely girl called Janine. We then spent the day seeing the entry into Jerusalem that Jesus rode, spent time in the old city, and joined in with the Feast of Tabernacles that evening, which was wonderful.

The next day we visited Bethlehem, toured Jerusalem and again went to the Feast of Tabernacles, which I was beginning to get some grasp of. 1980 was the first year ever that Gentiles had joined the Jews in the Feast of Tabernacles, fulfilling prophecy and answering much prayer. It was a significant time in history and sometimes one does not quite grasp the full meaning of what is actually happening in our midst.

The next day I was to join Faans' tour around Israel. It was fantastic, but again quite fast, and not giving enough time for so much to sink into one's mind.

The last day we were at Lake Galilee. I decided to get up at 5:00 am and walk up the hill behind the hotel to be alone for a while, as today I was to be baptised in the river Jordan by Faans Klopper. This was a big moment for me, for although I had been christened as a baby, I was now making my own decision on the matter.

I walked up and found a large rock near the top. The sun was just about to rise. I had my camera with me to take some slides of it and I did so. Then I grabbed some paper to write.

This is God's own land
Echoing with power and glory
Which only He can change
As she attracts people from all lands
And walks of life, to walk her timeless paths
She teaches them through the truth of history
Of her glorious creator
Who blessed her with His own Son.

So this is the land of Israel
Though her peoples have suffered long
Yet from this comes greater glory
Out of the deepest valley, the highest peak
Her people are climbing now
And oh the victory when they reach the top
And see for themselves what lies ahead
The promised new life, their Saviour, their Lord.

The sun was rising higher. I put my pen away and began to run down the grassy slopes and back to the hotel for breakfast. Straight after breakfast we caught a boat across Lake Galilee and I even had a go with the driving wheel. We arrived at a village on the other side and caught the bus to the Jordan River that flowed into it. I was wearing a swimming costume underneath, so I was all ready for the baptism.

I was surprised at how cold the water was and walked into it about waist deep. With everyone looking on, Faans also

Coming up out of the water at the baptism

walked in and came up to me. He said a prayer and then, pushing me backwards, baptised me.

I came up out of the water with my arms raised, and water in my nose, trying to comprehend the importance of the moment. Later I was to find out that it was a new beginning and new learning from God.

A lot of pruning lay ahead which produced a stronger faith in the Lord.

Faans decided that I should go onto Kibbutz Einat, as they were passing it on the way back to Jerusalem.

It looked quite a poor kibbutz, but the dining room looked nice and modern. Here Faans met a man who led me to a bomb shelter where the Christians on the kibbutz were able to meet. Faans gave me a letter from Janine, said goodbye and left.

I sat down and waited and waited. I then opened Janine's letter, grabbed my diary and wrote:

> 'At this moment I am sitting in a bomb shelter, the church of Kibbutz Einat. I have just arrived and will wait for David to show the way, in this new life.
>
> I have just opened a letter Janine sent me, and cried for such love expressed, not only in the beauty of the words but also in her gift of shekels, that God supplies every need.
>
> Praise God for people like Janine who radiate with God's love.'

David then came in, showed me around the kibbutz and then took me to my new room. This was a wooden shack with shower rooms some distance away, which 70 of us had to share. What really concerned me was that the showers had no curtains. I would have to shower very late at night, I decided.

He left me to settle in and I tried to dust and sweep, for there was a large hole in the ceiling which seemed to drop more dust than I had ever seen. The more I swept, the more dust there was. I shared the room with a Spanish girl, who could not speak a word of English. I was not sure at all about all this, but I was here for three months, so would have to make the best of it.

The next shock was supper. We only had bread and salad to eat, but at least I liked tomatoes and there were plenty of those.

Sunday, 5th October: At 5.00 am we all jumped into a very old jeep and drove out into the orange groves, where we had to weed around each orange tree by hand.

I thought, 'Well, we are just lucky that we can choose what we would like to be: either useless, like weeds, or yielded to service like fruit trees.'

We worked until 10.00 am and then went back to the Kibbutz for breakfast – salad again.

Monday, 6th October: I had to prune rose bushes. I was corrected for not pruning them down enough and was shown how to prune down to the thicker stem to produce larger roses. In some cases it was necessary to prune right down to the roots, but always to cut just above a new shoot and to choose a shoot that would grow outwards, not inwards, as this would cause problems.

I realised we too needed pruning. God prunes the bad branches out of our lives, that we too may produce better and bigger fruit for Him. Sometimes He too prunes us back to our roots, or back to square one, that we may grow again, stronger and thicker and more stable in our faith.

God also prunes us so that we may grow outwards to witness to the world what He has done for us. Even though the actual pruning may be painful, the end result is to God's glory – a tree that bears much fruit.

I realised God was pruning me and as my hands got thorns in them and scratched, I closed my eyes in repentance to God. I suddenly saw weeds in my life – lots of them: weeds of greed, self-will, pride, impatience. I handed them to God one by one, for Him to pluck them out of me.

The lady came back. 'That's OK,' she said. 'Now put manure around them,' and left.

So the rest of the time was spent doing just that. I completed the job on time, but felt exhausted in the hot sun.

As I walked back to my hut, I thought, 'Who am I, that God should teach me all this?'

He said to me, 'Did you not prune and manure every rose bush?'

'Yes,' I said, 'every rose bush is important.'

'So are you,' He said.

'Lord,' I responded, 'You are so good, better than everything there is. You make a rose to grow from a thorn bush. You even wore a crown of thorns on Your head. How much more, then, can you cause beauty to come forth from the human race and turn prickly people into Your own sons and daughters? And me? It's no use being prickly, I too must yield to pruning, and allow You to deal with me.'

Tuesday, 7th October: I was still pruning roses and learnt another hard lesson . . .

I see what I am really like. I want to run from the hard work, the heat, and sore muscles. In my old self, the natural self, I would have left this kibbutz already, but the choice is mine. God's blessing or no blessing. If God has brought me here for a definite purpose by His grace, I will stay for that purpose to come about. I mowed four lawns then went back to pruning and manuring roses.

I realise God is cleaning me up too and I don't like it, because I now see my faults. He is breaking me and I want to resist, but realise I have to yield to it fully and completely. This kibbutz is breaking me and though I am hating every bit of it, I thank God for it, for it's the only way I can really go ahead for God in a disciplined and completely yielded way, no matter what the task shall be.

Wednesday, 8th October: The bakery. Everyone in there became moulded together in the work. It was hot and noisy, and there were conveyer belts everywhere with people working hard to keep up with them. I had to bring in loads of boxes to pack the bread into.

I piled them up high and tried to carry them in like everyone else, but balancing them was not so easy. I just kept dropping the whole lot and collapsed into tears.

I thought, 'Yes, you're trying to balance your own life. Why not just trust in Jesus to help you? Stop worrying how long you can last out. Just trust.'

I pulled myself together, tried with fewer boxes and managed to complete the day's work with no further mishaps.

Thursday, 9th October: At 2.30 am I met with the night shift in the bakery on the conveyer belt. Well, I may be able to handle a runaway horse, but I was at a loss as to how to handle runaway buns! The bread tins stopped coming, but the buns just kept coming, and I had no tins to put them in. I piled them up high on the side of the table until a few tins came along. But trying to balance all the buns . . . sometimes two fell into one tin . . . then the tins stopped coming again, but the buns kept coming . . . I shouted, but no one heard. The piles of buns kept coming. Now they were falling all over me ... onto the dirty floor ... everywhere. By this time I was screaming, '**Help!**' Surely, this was some terrible nightmare! I tried to wake up, but I couldn't – **I was awake!** I was being buried alive, by buns! '**Help!**' I cried out again.

'It's OK. Don't cry – give you other job. Know how to plait bread?'

'No,' I cried.

He took my fingers and showed them how to do it. 'Just do that and that, and they are plaited.'

He left me to do 'that and that', and they were plaited. I had to concentrate to keep up with that murderous conveyor belt: I did not want runaway *shabbat* bread too. It took all my effort and concentration to do this job. I think I must have fallen asleep standing up, still plaiting bread and keeping up with that conveyor belt. When 6.00 am came, they could not get through to me to stop plaiting bread. I neither heard them nor felt them tapping on my shoulder to stop. Finally, at 8.00 am, the bread suddenly stopped coming and I woke up with a shock.

'You have worked two hours overtime,' someone said. 'You could not hear us telling you to stop.'

I walked outside into the hot sun, cried to my hut, fell into bed and slept.

I awoke about lunchtime. As it was my first day off, I did not want to waste it. I had an invitation to ride one of the two horses on the kibbutz, so I saddled up with an old military saddle and departed.

I had a super ride up to the ruined castle on top of the hill overlooking the kibbutz. Here I began to understand what this kibbutz was made of. The stony barren ground told me of endless hard work, horses put to plough, people living in wood shacks, details like dirt overlooked, and what had been accomplished to turn this area into a shady and prosperous kibbutz.

It had taken much team spirit and dedication to achieve what had been done here. A barren land had been transformed into fertile ground flowing with milk and honey: trees and shade, fruit and crops.

I then rode past the graveyard of the pioneers who had died here. In one way I felt sad as I thought about what it must have been like to have lived here all one's life and died here. But then I saw what had been accomplished here for the younger generation. Those old men must have been happy to see the fruit of their own hands prosper and the kibbutz flourishing under the care of their sons and daughters.

I myself had now had a taste of the hard work here and the dedication of fellow volunteers who had given up their own comfortable lives to come and serve these people. Why had they come? For no other reason than the call of God and the fulfilment of prophecy: *'Aliens shall stand and feed your flocks; foreigners shall be your ploughmen and vinedressers'* (Isaiah 61:5).

It takes more than a verbal commitment to God: it takes the sacrifice of one's life and hard physical effort. Just as these volunteers were laying down their lives in order to build up this kibbutz for their younger generation, so ought we to lay down our own lives, in hard physical effort, to show forth the love of God to His people. We then become the healing ointment to deep wounds of hate and persecution, which the Jews have suffered from so-called Christians.

We are known here as 'The believers', and this silent witness has already been received as Jews secretly believe and receive Jesus as their Messiah.

I thought, 'Can I give myself so fully to this work? Can I be as dedicated as these Christians, who surely love God more than mother, father, brother or sister? These people never speak about Jesus. All they do is live the life, and people notice the difference.'

Friday, 10th October: Life continued to be like the conveyor belt – sometimes OK, sometimes full of problem buns. Today the bakery was actually swept, and I was given the job of scrubbing tables, sinks, cupboards, etc. This was hard work with a cement trough, wire wool and scraper.

In the afternoon I ended up sitting in the middle of a peanut field, eating peanuts. It had been good fun collecting them with Michael and Ron, running through sprinklers, orchards and river beds, and we had also found a water melon, that had grown in the rubbish dump. Now for the peanut party.

I had a lovely time of fellowship that evening, and again I was struck deeply by the dedication of these believers. This group was really mature in the Lord. They also gave me a surprise birthday party and a couple of presents. I was so thrilled; I hardly knew what to say. We spoke of the possible war that might break out here. They would all stay on, for all the men would be called-up and the women would have to run the kibbutz. I realised, 'That is real testing. These believers are victorious in Christ; they are lovely people wholly dedicated, full of fun, yet serious in their mission.'

'I thought I was dedicated, but now, in comparison, I'm not so sure. I've found it harder than I ever imagined, having been drawn to tears a few times already by the pressure. Could I pull through? Would I survive this? Yes, I have to.'

Tearfully I looked down at my Bible and played with my pen, then I read some words that leapt out at me: *'Beloved do not be surprised at the fiery ordeal which comes upon you to prove you, as though something strange were happening to you, but rejoice in so far as you share Christ's sufferings that you may also rejoice and be glad when his glory is revealed'* (1 Peter 4:12).

I then felt unworthy before God, but I sensed that He was saying that as I might cry over the dirt of the bakery, so He cries over the sin in this world. Repent, clean it out, be as a fresh-baked loaf and God will bless you exceedingly.

Saturday, 11th October: I had a day off, so I went to a village called Roshia. It was here that the Yemenites who were rescued from Yamin by a great bird (actually a plane), as prophesied in Scripture, stayed. These Jews were dark-skinned, friendly and very religious, and some were praying out loud on their porches. Children also wore the small caps and went to Synagogue. They were very close-knit and the streets felt safe and peaceful.

Sunday, 12th October: I wanted to ride up into the hills and I was allowed to take the stallion. I sat down to rest at an ancient well; Bedouin on donkeys were driving some cattle down the hill.

My thoughts went to John 4:13: Jesus said, *'Everyone who drinks of this water will thirst again but whoever drinks of the water that I shall give him will never thirst. The water that I shall give him will become in him a spring of water welling up to eternal life.'*

I suddenly felt He was speaking to me: 'My living waters have gone forth; be as a living well to these people. I need many wells to make available My living waters to My people.'

Monday, 13th October: I had a struggle, and I lacked the courage to get through the two shifts: 10.00 am to 4.00 pm and 10.30 pm to 2.00 am. In the bakery I was given the job of lifting trays of bread from the oven to racks at top speed. This was too heavy for me, and I cried at my failure. They were kind to me, and put me onto scrubbing machinery instead.

The afternoon went much better and I was thrilled to hear that they had closed the bakery down for three days to clean it out. As we scraped years of dirt off machinery, I realised God was speaking through even that. As we chiselled off thick grease, took machinery apart for cleaning, and cleaned out all the corners, the bakery began to take on a new freshness.

This applied not only to what God was doing in my life, but also to the whole nation. If they would come to a place of repentance, then God would clean out years of hurt, unforgiveness, hate and hard grime, and suddenly the freshness of His Holy Sprit would blow over this land in new life.

Tuesday, 14th October: I thought back to my baptism and the testings since then. I had not realised at the time that we too go through a wilderness experience after baptism, when God works within us and prepares us for Christian living.

Today I was to work in the dining room. The shifts were much easier, so I did my best, and stayed on to finish off when the clock indicated it was time to leave.

Wednesday, 15th and Thursday, 16th October: I also worked in the dining room on Wednesday, as I finished off the work after time, an old man called me over, put down his paper and said, 'Why do you stay on to finish the work when everyone else has left?'

'To finish the job,' I replied.

'And what else?' he went on.

'I suppose,' I said 'it's because I am a Christian and want to do a good job.'

'Sit down,' he said. 'Tell me about yourself.'

I sat down and answered many questions.

Then, getting up, he said, 'Will you come and tell me more about your Jesus tomorrow?'

'With pleasure,' I said, and went home.

Isaac had given me some homework to do. He had asked me why the Jews had to suffer so much. After asking the other believers, I came back with a satisfactory answer.

Friday, 17th October: I plucked up enough courage to give Isaac the book I had written, *Search for Truth,* which he accepted gladly.

That night the new English group had a wild party, played with Ouija boards, got drunk and broke up many flowers in the dining-room gardens.

Saturday, 18th October: I had another day off, so I went for a walk with Ron up into the hills. All the believers were fasting, so I joined in as well.

Ron got a word from the Lord, which was almost the same as I had received a week ago. This was wonderful confirmation for me.

That evening I had just got into my hut, when the Holy Spirit prompted me to go down to the bomb shelter. 'But there's no meeting planned!' I stalled, but felt I had to go anyway. To my surprise every one of us was arriving at the same time and, without a word, went straight into prayer.

Truly God's presence was there in power. We prayed against the evil that had caused so much ugliness in last night's party. We banned the area of the Ouija boards, etc.

After a time, we were suddenly set free to worship and we almost shouted our praise forth in tongues. Being in God's presence like this is the greatest joy on earth and praising Him is glorious. An hour or so later, a holy silence came over us and we began to leave, almost afraid to speak, knowing we had met with God.

Our leaders went out first and met Jews who had been listening.

'Why were you praying like that?' they asked, 'What's happened? That's how the religious Jews in Jerusalem pray when someone dies and we did not know you could speak classical Hebrew.'

Our leaders explained, and the Jews went home relieved and amazed, especially as not one of us could speak much Hebrew, let alone classical Hebrew.

The result of that glorious prayer meeting was amazing. No more trouble with the English group and they even complained that their Ouija board would not work anymore.

I was beginning to see and feel the reality of Jesus in our midst. This was both awesome as well as comforting. Awesome, because of imperfections in our lives; comforting, because of His closeness to us.

I thought back to Friday ... 'An olive tree full of olives in the wilderness, then later a fig tree full of sweet black figs, then later still a cactus also with red fruit. So this barren land, does bear fruit.'

Then I thought of the believers, alone and isolated as they die to worldly pleasures and comfort, and become reborn in the Holy Spirit of God ... 'The overflow is like seeds of newborn faith in another being, who also grows in Christ and reaches yet others.'

Sunday, 19th October: I worked on the cotton fields.

Monday, 20th October: I worked in the bakery. Only God can make sweeping into a satisfying and rewarding job. While I was going to extra lengths brushing under and behind machinery – whoops – I realised someone was coming to turn it on. I began to push his foot hard with the broom, causing him to leap back in alarm and I kept moving the broom until he realized I was under the machine, so narrowly escaping being minced up.

Wednesday, 22nd October: The bakery again. I felt as if my endurance was coming to an end and kept quoting *'Those who wait upon the Lord shall renew their strength.'* Thinking that maybe I was not waiting on God enough, I awoke thirty minutes early to do just that – at least it kept me from crying.

At breakfast old Mr Isaac came up and said, 'The Book, the psalms, *Search for Truth,* you gave me, I have received Him, of whom that book speaks, into my heart.'

Because of the light in his face I could believe it. He had met with the Lord, and I praised God for this. For Isaac to have met with Jesus made all this worthwhile.

Thursday, 23rd October: In the morning, I asked the Lord why Isaiah 40:31 did not work for me, for it said, *'But they who wait for the Lord shall renew their strength, they shall mount up with wings like eagles, they shall run and not be weary, they shall walk and not faint.'* The Lord led me to Mark 6:43: *'And they took up twelve baskets-full of broken pieces and of fish.'*

It did not make sense. I asked the Lord, 'The overflow – this was the overflow from the miracle of feeding the 5,000. So does this mean I must wait on You till I overflow? If so, how?'

The Lord led me to John 4:23: *'But the hour is coming and now is it when the true worshippers will worship the Father in spirit and truth, for such the Father seeks to worship Him.'*

'Lord,' I said. 'I can worship in truth but how do I worship in Spirit to overflowing?'

I knelt down and suddenly the Lord showed me how. He brought me into a new dimension of worship and I did not want to stop – but I had to go to work. Anyway, it says in the Bible, *'Pray without ceasing.'*

I went to work at the bakery again, but I was so busy worshipping the Lord silently and inwardly, that I hardly noticed the hard work outwardly.

'What's happened to you?' asked one of the bosses. 'I've never seen you work so easily and so happily.'

From that day forward I have never again been brought to tears by hard work. I had learnt the conditions of Isaiah 40: 'Through prayer, God will feed us with His love and out of the overflow we can then feed others.' All Scripture works, if we fulfil the conditions. Serving God is not a project, but un overflow: waiting on God produces the overflow.

That evening at a prayer meeting in the bomb shelter, there was also a prophecy, 'that when the sun broke through black clouds, then I was to leave.'

From then on I had no further difficulties with the work. The prophecy about clouds seemed far away though, for I not yet even seen a cloud in the sky.

Being able to handle the work more easily also meant that there was energy left for other things, like touring.

One of the first outings was to Antipatris, where Paul was kept prisoner on his way to Caesarea (Acts 23:31).

It was an ancient old fort, and I decided I also wanted to see the dungeon where Paul was kept prisoner. It was cold, damp and dark with only a narrow slit for a window. On the floor was an old fallen pillar, so I went to sit down and absorb the sight. I got out my pen and paper and wrote:

The sunray pierced deep, onto the dark dungeon floor
A narrow streak of light, with beauty in its touch
Is this what Paul went through, persecuted by many men
To stay here a while, a prisoner of mankind?

It's the sunray that spoke to me
Of the glory of God's light
The narrow streak of hope
With wonder in its touch

Is this what helped Paul through
When suffering alone
To wait on God of high
For wisdom how to write?

It's the wisdom of God's light
That revealed him the truth
The narrow streak of light
With power in its touch

The overflow of God's love
That helped Paul, write the Epistles
To reveal to the whole world
The salvation of our Lord

Like the wisdom of God's light
That escaped those prison walls
The gospel was sent forth
With heaven in its touch.

I was reminded of John 7:37–38 when on the great, last day of the feast, Jesus stood up and proclaimed: *'if anyone thirst, let him come to me and drink. He who believes in me as the Scripture has said, out of his heart shall flow rivers of living waters.'*

I thought, 'No one could stop a river: it would just crash through, or race over, or around the top. And the nearer to the sea it gets, the wider it becomes. And this scripture spoke of rivers, not just one river.'

I looked back over the poem I had just written. Not even these dungeon walls could stop the rivers of living waters flowing forth from Paul's life, for it was in dungeons like this that Paul wrote most of his letters to the churches to form part of the Bible.

'How many lives have been changed through this one man, back then and during nearly 2000 years since?' I wondered.

I looked at my own life, barely a trickle in comparison. And I was free – no dungeons or chains to deal with.

I felt very challenged by this visit to Paul's dungeon, and took a last breath of the musty damp air before getting up. I took a last look round feeling as though I had been touched and taught by the Lord Himself. I felt humbled, for that writing was not of me and had taught me much.

Monday, 27th October: the next day. I worked in the bakery cleaning machinery. Chris worked with me and we spoke about the Lord for nearly an hour.

After Bible study that evening, I went for a walk near the horses and cows and sat down a while. The Kibbutz lights were shining from different angles, causing shadows all around me: before me, beside me and behind me as I stood up. I had been thanking the Lord for all He was teaching me at this kibbutz and felt His beautiful love around me and within me.

'Go, and stay in My presence
And I will stay with you
Before you to prepare the way
Behind you to protect the way
Beside you to guide the way.'

I praised God.

Tuesday, 28th October: The Lord was not finished with me yet. He had still more to show me and teach me.

'Can anyone here drive?'

I put my hand up.

'Come.'

I climbed up into the large tractor, looking quizzically at the gears. After a little thought, I put it into first gear, causing a muffled grind, and slowly pulled off.

'Looks like I've got the job,' I thought.

'Hey, stop!' I heard, and stamped down the clutch.

Stones came whirling into the trailer from six volunteers, who were clearing stones from the cotton field.

I inched slowly forward: stop ... go ... stop ... go ... The trailer was soon full, and I put on a little gas. Suddenly the front wheels reared up from the ground. 'Hey!' I shouted, as all the steering became useless. The wheels descended back down to earth, but only for a second, before again lifting even higher in the air, because of the weight of the stones filling the two-wheel trailer.

I now had to go and dump the stones, but was not too sure how to keep the front wheels on the ground. Luckily a big, strong man came to help and with the weight of both of us, we were able to steer to the river dump.

'Trying to steer your own life? Why not consult the Lord?' echoed through my brain.

'Well, why can't I steer my own life?' I thought. 'Could it be that, like the trailer, my life was weighed down by too many activities or problems? Was I racing ahead with all direction lost?' I recalled that it was only when the man got in with me, that the wheels stayed on the ground. 'Are You saying something to me, Lord?'

Yes, He was. The Lord had said last night that He would be beside me to guide the way.

The lesson: God cannot be beside us unless we ask for His help and guidance; but when we do, then He will 'keep our front wheels on the ground', and only through this, will we be able to steer through this life, correctly guided and in His perfect will.

Wednesday, 29th October: I had still more to learn and had the most wonderful day. After having worked until midnight in the bakery and then helping with the delivery of a still-born calf, I decided to spend Wednesday, my day off, going to Tel Aviv and Joppa.

Carolyn, one of the English group whom we had prayed for in the bomb shelter, came with me. I wanted to visit the house of Simon the Tanner where Peter saw the vision of the unclean foods in Acts 10:11. Carolyn and I walked up the stairs onto the roof and sat down on one of the two rounded domes. From here we looked out to sea at small wooden fishing boats that could not have changed much since Peter's time.

I opened my Bible to read Acts 10:11.

'Read it aloud so I can also hear it,' asked Carolyn.

I did so, and went on to the part where the Holy Spirit fell on the Gentiles also.

'Tell me about the Holy Spirit,' asked Carolyn.

I explained how Jesus had sent His Holy Spirit to dwell in our hearts after His resurrection, how the Holy Spirit came upon the disciples as tongues of fire on the day of Pentecost, and how they then went out to do the same miracles as Jesus had done, causing the Church to come into being.

'Is Jesus really true then?' she asked.

'Of course,' I said.

'Can I also become a Christian and receive the Holy Spirit then?' she asked.

'Yes you can. I could pray for you right now if you like.'

'Please do,' she said, and closed her eyes.

I prayed, with Carolyn praying out loud after me. We prayed that He would forgive our sins, come into Carolyn's life as Lord and Saviour and also baptise her in the Holy

Spirit. Suddenly the Holy Spirit came down on both of us in the most wonderful blessing and anointing. Half-an-hour later we were still praising the Lord, filled with the joy of the Holy Spirit. The Lord seemed to say to me that the miracles were not only for the disciples of that day, but just as powerful for this day as well. Never will we forget those precious moments with the Lord.

At that moment, Zechariah came up the steps to see why we were taking so long, as he wanted to close up and visit his son. On the way down the steps we told him of the wonderful experience we had just had with the Lord and he was amazed. After shaking hands with him, we left. We then did some shopping, bought my mother a gift and returned to the kibbutz. Later that day Carolyn came with me to the Bible study.

The rest of the week went smoothly and on Saturday, Rindhard and I walked far into the hills of Samaria. We came to the place called Izbet Sarta Eben Ezar near the Canaanite Philistine village of Aphek mentioned in 1 Samuel 4, where the battle between the Israelites and Philistines took place. The Israelites were defeated and the Ark of the Covenant captured. Some years later it was again occupied by the Jews, after David drove the Philistines out of Izbet Sarta, but is now abandoned.

I started thinking ... 'So David walked these very hills ...'

Walk this rocky ground
Feel the stones beneath your feet
Brush through the yellow grass
Look at the endless hills.

It's here you meet with God
With your sacrifice of praise
And wait on Christ the King
Rest in His perfect love.

It's here where David walked
His Psalms are in your hand
He knew how to praise God
His writings show you how.

So lift your eyes to God
And praise His Holy name
He is King of kings
He is Lord of lords.

'Come now, we've got to get back,' called Reinhard.

I put my pen away and enjoyed a gorgeous sunset walk back to the kibbutz.

A few days later, Tuesday 4th November, a very amazing thing happened. I was walking with three other believers to post some letters when suddenly a Jewish girl came running up crying, shouting, 'Jeshua,' and hugged one of the men.

'What's wrong?' we asked.

'Nothing,' she replied. 'I'm so happy. I've just seen Jesus.'

'How?' we asked.

'Oh,' she said. 'Come back to my appartment, and I will tell you.'

We walked back with her and she explained how she had seen the trailer of *Jesus of Nazareth.*

'I know what Jesus looks like from there,' she went on. 'And I saw a vision of that same face in this man, so I know Jesus is true. Will you pray for me?'

So we led her to the Lord, and the Lord touched her deeply, healing her of many hurts and problems.

We were so filled with wonder at God's love and the different ways He uses to call His people to Himself. I simply had to write the following:

The Healer

She was lost in utter darkness
Worries look over her mind
This brought her nerves to breaking
She was broken, utter despair

She fumbled to find the way
But confusion puzzled her mind
What has she, but to give up
And crawl an aimless path

Then one day it happened
A light shone in her path
She looked to where it came
And saw Jesus Christ the Lord

She got up on her feet
She raised her arms in praise
And the Healer of creation
Sent her dancing on her way.

The Lord is so, so wonderful and I was learning more and more about Him.

Listen to the Lord in the silence and He will direct you. Rest in Him alone, living for today and the calmness of your mind shall open the way to God's voice.

Come silently before Him, rest in Him and He shall direct the desires of your heart, as you live to please Him.

Chapter 18

New Horizons – Cyprus

I was working in the bakery again. Full of energy, I got through the work quickly and went to ask what else needed to be done.

'Nothing,' came the reply. 'Go for a walk or something, and come back in half-an-hour.'

So I took a walk out in to the cotton fields.
The Black clouds swirled across the hills
Bringing the world into a strange and lonely darkness
Then the wind blew rain in slanting lines
Which sank fast into the thirsty ground.

Suddenly the rain stopped and a quiet came over all, the sweet smell of rain remaining unmoved. Then, as I looked, there came a parting in the clouds.

I ran over to where a long narrow streak of sunlight was moving across the cotton fields. It was so narrow that when I stood in its long, narrow streak, my own shadow blocked off the light where I was standing, causing me to be covered in sunlight instead. I turned round and watched this silver thread of sunlight struggling up the hills and finally reaching the very top. Not that the final conquest of the light was important, but rather its unending effort to achieve it. 'That's what life is about,' I thought. 'Unending effort to succeed or achieve, or simply to become a better person.'

All of a sudden this narrow streak of sunlight began to widen more and more, enveloping the village, then the Arab villages and Petah Tikva. A breeze then came up and gently pushed me forward and at that moment I felt the presence of God come upon me: 'Move ahead.'

The sun had come through the clouds, the clouds had parted, the prophecy over me had come true. I felt a breakthrough into what God had ahead for me, and I rejoiced.

I had actually almost completed my stay, with only a couple of weeks to go. That night we had some visitors at our Bible study from Cyprus and they invited me to stay with them for a week. I was very excited. They were part of Youth With A Mission.

Next day I went to book my tickets to Cyprus and Greece. I got a bit nervous, but it seemed to me that I was to cast my bread upon the waters, so I went ahead and booked.

I had also made friends with some lovely people who ran the Baptist village about 30 minutes walk from the kibbutz. I had begun attending the 'Southern Baptist Church' on most Saturday mornings and had gone on a lovely church trip to Jerusalem with them. They now invited me to work for them on my return from Greece and I was thrilled to accept their offer.

All just seemed to fit into place. The Lord had taught me so much at Kibbutz Einat, especially about prayer and coming into His presence daily. Here He had soaked me in His love until I could hardly sit still, wanting to leap with praise instead. Such precious moments with the Lord just make your spirit fly with song.

'No wonder everyone in the Dining Room keeps asking me why I'm so happy – who couldn't be?' I thought. 'It's not me that makes me happy, but the Lord.'

I worked mostly in the bakery that week, and then on Friday the 14th got ready for a kibbutz trip to the Sinai.

We all piled into the kibbutz bus and had a long interesting trip: down past the Dead Sea, through the desert, across the border and along the side of the Red Sea to Corral Island, where we stopped.

After a supper of bread, tomatoes and salad, we unrolled our sleeping bags and slept on the beach.

At the first signs of dawn next morning, I was up and climbed the hill behind the beach. This was not easy, as the slates from the slate rocks kept giving way under my feet, but I made it before sunrise.

I sat down to watch the sunrise over Coral Island with its ancient fort. It was silent, but not quite. The desert breeze seemed to blow through the dry sands and over its rocky slates. I grabbed my pen: I had a song to write to its tune.

The Desert Breeze

Blow like the desert breeze
That combs this barren land
Giving the Spirit of Christ
As water to the thirsty soul

Rise like the everlasting sun
Bringing light, into the day
Sharing the word of Christ
That shows the way to go

Walk this desert land
Caring for all that you meet
Living the word of Christ
Showing the salvation of God

The lonely wind shall praise you
Lifting up its desert song
Whispering 'I love You'
To the everlasting God

So let's lift up our praise
With this wind that blows
Lifting up our worship
To the everlasting God.

That day we rode camels, went to the aquarium to see fish of all colours, and went snorkelling at Oasis. I bought some saddlebags. That night we slept on the beach again.

Next morning, Sunday 16th, I went for an early morning walk and saw a lone camel at a water hole. He seemed to want some water, so I tried to draw some water for him. This was not so easy, for I could not get the tin to sink. The camel nudged me and breathed down my neck. I then tried throwing the tin in upside down. That worked, and I pulled the tin up with some water in it, which the camel slurped down.

After breakfast some Bedouin invited us in for some very sweet tea, and one of the them sang us a song, accompanied by his one-stringed guitar.

We then drove home, stopping for a while on the way at a game reserve kibbutz on the Dead Sea. It had been a good trip.

There was now only one week left before leaving all alone for Cyprus and Greece. I was a little fearful, but God was to speak to me:

'Be not afraid to follow Me, neither draw back in doubt, for I will pave the way for you with My bounty. You are not treading alone. No, there are many with you on the same road. It is the road of faith and trust and you shall have sweet fellowship, for there are others who shall join you in this walk. You shall rejoice with exceeding joy and the joy shall be shared by angels, as they walk beside you to guard the way.'

I was filled with awe.

On Saturday, the day before leaving for Cyprus, I had a wonderful day in Jerusalem. As I passed through Arab villages, I saw donkeys ploughing, village life, and beautiful hill country. Then on up to Mount Zion, spending the rest of day in the old city and at the Wailing Wall.

On Sunday I caught the bus to Haifa. I did not want to travel alone, but it seemed that I would be. Suddenly, as I was queuing up to get my passport stamped, the man in front of me said to me, 'You are a Christian.'

'How do you know?' I replied.

'I can see it on your face,' he replied.

'Then you must be one too,' I answered.

'Sure,' he replied.

'Where are you travelling to?' I asked.

'The YWAM base in Cyprus,' he replied.

'So am I,' I blurted out. 'What's your name?' I asked.

'David,' he replied. 'And yours?'

'Suzanne.'

'Well, let's travel together,' he invited.

'Fine by me,' I replied.

We got onto the ship together and went to the deck where we were to travel. There were two dormitories with hammocks, one for the ladies and one for the gents. The next morning we arrived at Cyprus. I found David to travel with to the YWAM base, which was just as well, for we had to hire a taxi and he knew how to get there. I would have got totally lost.

The YWAM base was high up in the hills. We got out of the taxi and went to the office. The staff showed us to where we would be staying, taking me to my room first, and left me to settle in. There was a welcome card on my bed, along with three red flowers. I picked up the card and opened it. 'Welcome to Cyprus,' it said. 'We are so glad you are here. With love, YWAM CYPRUS.' There was also a scripture from 1 John 5:11. I was thrilled with it and then went to find the others. I was immediately welcomed as one of them and the love shown to me and to each other was like a ministry in itself. So I joined in everything with them. The lectures we attended every morning were exactly what I needed most, helping me to understand people with different personalities.

Each day started at 6.30 am with breakfast, and continued as follows: 7.00 am – quiet time; 8.00 am – block groups; 10.00 am – lectures; 1.00 pm – lunch; 2.00 pm – work; 6.00 pm – supper; 7.30 pm – lectures; 10.30 pm – quiet time and bed.

I learnt that to be a great worker for God you must be a great worshipper, that a ministry was anything that blesses others, and that your effectiveness in ministry will be as powerful as your time alone with the Lord.

In the afternoons I helped bake homemade bread, and assisted in the kitchen and dining room. We also had time off.

Saturday, 29th November: The sun's rays broke through the clouds, highlighting the hills with long strips of sunlight. It was harvest and Cypriot women were busy at work in the olive groves, picking and sorting olives.

It was a good harvest, with old and young working together joyfully,

Further along the fields, Diogenes was out with his goats, his snow-white moustache and hair shining in the sun. He too was joyful, swinging his long stick as he strode along, wearing gumboots, wide breeches and coat.

Katydata was quiet. I walked gaily through narrow cobbled streets, past a young girl tending her garden and mud-bricked homes with wooden balconies, to Skevi Loizidon's home on the hill.

What a welcome! Soon we were chatting in her lounge. Skevi's brother had just arrived home from his studies. After a short time her mom, aunt and grandmother returned from the olive groves, and touched me on the cheek as a sign of welcome. They then went to change, as the church bells had already begun to ring.

'A bit of a rush tonight,' Skevi told me. 'The vicar wants to see the film tonight, so they are having church an hour early.'

Having changed, mom picked up her basket of prepared bread and juice for St Andrew's Day. The rest of us finished our Turkish coffee, then together we ventured out into the rain. I walked as far as the church with them, then said goodbye. As I gaily ran off in the rain, I met more villagers on their way to the church who waved to me. Soon I was running across the fields with water streaming down my face.

Raise your hands to God
Dance your praise to Him
As a child shakes his wet hair
And goats run glad and free

Sunday, 30th November: I had another wonderful day walking through the villages. Everyone was so friendly and we talked to them: about the olive press ... the lady on her donkey... I spoke to a lady making sausages, then her children walked with me to get some keys from a friend and proudly showed me their beautiful village church. Outside it an aged Cypriot man, who had recently lost his wife, had shaved his head and was mourning. He looked so sad, so lonely and hungry that we gave him a pound. He cried with gratitude and we then prayed to God together, which cheered him up quite a bit. While walking back with the children, they assured me that the villagers would look after him.

After that I got invited in for tea and cake. Right next to the home was an old brick building filled with hay. Next to that was a cow, and a waiting donkey, still with its harness on.

After this we all walked down to another village to buy groceries. My two friends, with their mother and aunt, popped into visit a friend on the way back and we were all invited in for juice and delicious cakes.

The new friends we had made would not allow us to walk back to YWAM in the dusk, so they drove us to the base and we then went to visit Bill. Sunset concluded the wonderful visit to this ideal dreamlike community, where crime is unknown and the Christian church guides their daily lives. Praise God.

The YWAM base was also incredibly peaceful and the love shown to me was so warm and friendly in every way. The whole base was so pure and clean and filled with the righteousness of God. Even though established here for only three years, God was blessing YWAM abundantly and working through them mightily. During the week I learnt a tremendous amount and really became part of the team; so much so that I was asked to join the outreach team to Egypt. However, I had already paid for my ticket to Greece, and sadly had to decline.

The friendship we had was such that they even offered to drive David and me down to the docks to meet our ship the following day.

Chapter 19

Greece

YWAM took us right into the harbour, then said goodbye and drove off. We took our tickets out and went to get them stamped.

'Very sorry,' the ticket officer said, 'but you have missed your boat.'

'I can't have,' I retorted.

'Sorry, but it left an hour ago.'

'It can't have,' I repeated.

'Look,' he said, 'the *Arion* is going in half-an-hour. Give me 65 dollars and you can go on that one.'

'But I've only got 85 dollars,' I replied.

'That's more than enough,' he went on. 'That leaves you 20 dollars change.'

There was nothing else to do, so I paid the extra cost of the ticket and followed David onto the *Arion*.

'Oh well, I'll just have to fast,' I thought, trying to work out how I could possibly live on 20 dollars for a whole week in Greece.

The *Arion* was actually a better boat than the one we had missed; it even had beds to sleep in. I put my belongings onto the bed, and went out on deck.

My mind went back to Israel when, through a book, God had taught me: 'though cliffs should rise before you, there will always be provision and in My mercy I shall see that you find it. Do not let circumstances hold you, but rather control them. Never let anyone know your need.'

I did not tell anyone, of course, and decided a two-day fast would not harm me. However God supplied. A Greek man came to sit beside me. Without asking me he had ordered a delicious cheese, tomato and meat roll with Turkish coffee and set it before me. I did not realise I was so hungry and inwardly I praised God.

The same night a delicious dinner was supplied in a similar way: a meal ticket was put into my hand and I was invited to join a group for dinner. Praise God.

I had thought I had moved out of God's will by missing my boat, yet all I saw was God's provision in every aspect.

I prayed, 'Lord, You alone are my security and my strength. Sometimes my desires to see Your lands may run away with me, but in truth I do want to do as You would have me do. Please, Lord, do not allow me to go out of Your will.'

He said to me, 'Have faith and believe, do not strive, or you will limit Me. Rest in Me and be. That is all I ask you. Rest in me and be and I shall use you to My glory.'

I responded, 'Praise You, Lord. Thank you, Lord; I know that You are with me.'

On Tuesday we sailed into Rhodes and visited the beautiful old city. I bought a little bit of food, but again that evening I was invited to a wonderful dinner and this opened up a time of sharing how I came to know Jesus as Lord.

The next morning I took a photo of the sunrise over the Greek islands. The boat then pulled into the Greek harbour in Piraeus, a very large city with fruit-bearing orange trees lining the streets.

I felt a bit nervous again. I did not like cities. How was I going to live in this city for a whole week on so little money; not even enough for one night's stay in a youth hostel?

The ship was now coming into dock; I took my hand-luggage and went out onto the top deck. I had not seen David since we had come on board and I began to feel very alone. Not sure where to go, I just stood and looked.

All of a sudden, a very tall American man shouted, 'Hey there, my YWAM friends!'

I almost ran towards him in the crowd and followed him, not too closely, for I did not want him to notice me. He went straight up to the group he had shouted to and began to exchange greetings. I put my luggage down as close to them as I dared and watched them in silence. Then one of them looked towards me, came over, picked up my hand-luggage and began to walk with the others. I followed – now very close behind. They all stopped at a bus stop and a few minutes later we all got onto the bus. I simply asked for the same ticket as the others and sat down with them. I didn't have the faintest idea where we were going, but at least we were leaving the big city of Parys.

Less than an hour later we entered a small village called Eleousis, where there were docks, and we got off the bus.

'Be here in an hour and we will take the trawler over to the ship *Anastasias*,' said one of the group.

'Thank you so much,' I replied.

They then disappeared somewhere and I decided to visit the ancient ruins in the village, which dated from the Bronze Age to the time Paul introduced Christianity.

One hour later I was back. The others appeared a few minutes later and we boarded the trawler.

We spluttered towards the ship in the old, noisy trawler. The *Anastasias* was white and magnificent, perfectly reflected by the black waters, and shining like the ship of God against the black rain clouds. A ship with a mission: to bring the light of Christ to the world.

What a welcome awaited as we boarded it! Love from every side, as we entered the clean luxury of an ocean liner – a village of its own of believers aboard this ship giving love and care to every detail.

'The steward would like to see you,' I was told. 'He is in his office over there.'

'Thank you,' I replied and walked over to his office.

'Come in, and sit down.'

I walked in, put down my hand-luggage and sat down.

'Where do you come from?' he asked.

'South Africa,' I answered.

'Oh yes. We have quite a few South Africans on board; we will introduce you to them. And,' he went on, 'where have you just come from?'

'Israel,' I replied.

'And how long are you in Greece for?', he enquired.

'One week,' I replied.

'Yes, sounds right.' he said. 'Well, would you like the job?' he asked.

'What job?' I enquired.

'In the galley,' he replied, 'on dining-room duty.'

'I would love it,' I answered.

'Well, it's yours for the week.'

'Thank you so much,' I replied, feeling very relieved.

He called someone, and said to her, 'Show her to her cabin.'

I was shown to my cabin with its own bathroom and shower, and there on the table was a welcome card and a champagne glass filled with sweets, nuts and raisins. I cried with gratitude, picked up the card and opened it. It had a picture of a trawler, and read, 'Welcome aboard *MV Anastasias*', then the scripture, *'I am the resurrection and the life. He who believes in me shall live even if he dies'* (John 11:25) and 'we are happy that you have come to visit us. From the *Anastasias* family.'

'What if they have picked up the wrong person?' I thought. 'I must own up.'

I left everything there and went up and down the ship to find the people whom I had arrived with. At last I found one.

'Thank you so much for picking me up,' I said, 'but I had made no arrangements to come here.'

'Oh that,' he said. 'No, you are the right person, don't worry. You see, the lady who normally works in the galley and her husband who works on the decks are going to the mainland for a week, so that she can have her baby.

'So we were praying at the 6.30 am prayer meeting this morning for two people to replace them and do their jobs for the week. Then there was a prophecy in tongues from the old white-haired lady you saw when we came in, and the interpretation was, "Go down to the docks at 11.30 and you will find your two helpers for the week."

'So we obeyed, saw the two of you and brought you both back with us.

'By the way, you are both invited to the shower party for the Grasoons tonight. They will be leaving for the mainland in the morning. Come, it's time for supper.'

So I sat with his group and after a good supper we went to the shower party. Literally showers of gifts 'showered' upon her by the community. It was quite overwhelming.

I thought, 'The loving beauty of this community is getting through to me and changing me. Everywhere in the three different countries I've visited, the love of Christians towards each other has been the same – a far greater love than I've ever comprehended.'

> The love of God passes all understanding,
> I lift my eyes to God.
> Everywhere I go, His love is to be seen,
> Everywhere I look, His love is manifest.
> Everywhere I am, His love surrounds me still,
> I believe in this loving God,
> And lift my eyes to Him,
> And will always follow Him.

I prayed, 'Lord, teach me to show forth Your love to others, as others show forth Your love to me.'

The next morning I went down into the galley and they were making pancakes with syrup for breakfast. I helped lay the tables and, after a sweet pancake breakfast, helped with clearing-up, cleaning the dining room and setting the tables ready for lunch. We then had a break until an hour before supper, and ended the day an hour after supper – quite a pleasant job.

During the night I awoke at 3.00 am to a storm at sea, with the wind blowing very strongly and lightning flashing. Eventually, I went back to sleep and next morning I helped clean up after the storm, as rain had leaked through all the portholes in the dining room. Setting the cutlery for lunch was also impossible, as every time the ship swayed from side to side, all the cutlery landed on the floor.

I joined them for the 6.00 pm devotions. They wanted to send a Volkswagen of clothing to help victims of an earthquake that had happened in Italy the night before, and we prayed for the necessary permission from the authorities to do this.

That night it was still very stormy and by 10.00 pm the ship was in blackness.

Everywhere I looked I felt surrounded by blackness: the sea was wild and black, the coast was black and the winds were howling horribly, causing the ship to sway at awkward angles in the swells. I didn't like it, and I wasn't looking forward to three days on a smaller boat in such weather, going back to Israel.

I got into bed. One minute I was almost standing up and the next, nearly standing on my head. 'If the boat rocks any further,' I thought, 'it will sink.' I got back out of bed, put on my dressing gown and decided to go upstairs for a life-jacket. 'Just in case . . . ' I thought.

I took my little red torch and tried to balance myself as I went up the staircase into the lounge where I had seen them. Illuminated by candles, there was a meeting going on. I crept to the top of the stairs.

'No money had arrived at that time,' I overheard, 'but the refugees really needed it, so we decided to give up on our main meal for the three weeks and put our money towards it. Then suddenly the money came.'

'How much for?' asked another.

'1,224.00 dollars.'

My hair stood up on my head. That was the cheque I sent: the exact amount!

'Lord, forgive me,' I cried. 'I kept that money back. I caused these lovely people to do without their main meal for three weeks. It took me three weeks to obey You. Will You forgive me?'

I forgot about the life-jackets; I deserved to die anyway. I felt emptied out; I felt I was the worst person. I could never own up to them that I was that terrible person who had caused them to miss their main meal for three weeks, because of my disobedience to the voice of God.

I crept back to my cabin, and up into the swaying bed, heaving towards my feet, then heaving back towards my head. Every part of the ship was creaking. This was a horrible night. I grabbed my Bible and opened it at random, shining my torch onto the words: *'and he said to them, Why are you afraid O men of little faith? Then he stood up and rebuked the winds and the sea and there was a great calm'* (Matthew 8:26).

I thought, 'The power of the Word of God: it's as though Jesus is right here on this ship and has just woken up. He is so close; He is even within me.' I cried with relief. He had calmed my fears. I then cried because of my little faith and my fear. It was as if He had just rebuked my fears and dreads and there was a great calm.

I was also overwhelmed by His love and forgiveness: that He should forgive me for my disobedience and then still forgive me for my lack of faith all at the same time. I also realized that God had met every need on this trip. He had brought me onto this beautiful ship and was teaching me so much about walking in faith, about His wonderful love, about abiding in Him, and trusting Him.

I thought, 'For though blackness shall fall upon the earth – wars, earthquakes, floods, famines, antichrist – those who trust in God and keep their faith will be saved, and we, as believers, have a mission: for the harvest is ripe, but the labourers are few.'

Saturday was my day off, so I set off to ancient Corinth with some honey on bread for lunch. God again supplied every need: a lift to Corinth, where I bought some film and then caught the bus to ancient Corinth – a beautiful village. I took pictures of snow-capped mountains, sheep and donkeys and then had an enjoyable climb up the mountain to the ancient fort. After a wonderful time up there I met two Christians who offered me a lift down. We arrived in time to see the museum and ancient city before they brought me right back to the dock in good time for the trawler.

I had no sooner got aboard the *Anastasias* than it was time to leave again with the outreach team for Ephesus, where we met with success. God truly worked that night in the lives of a couple of young people there.

On Sunday we went to Athens for a Bible study and church, after which we were invited out for a delicious American lunch before returning at 4.00 pm. I attended another church service that night on the ship. It was another wonderful day.

Monday, the 8th: I was working in the galley, outwardly getting on with the job and enjoying the music, and inwardly communicating with God. The other day the same thing had happened. I was asked a question, and immediately it seemed as though the inward me was released by God's Spirit. He had opened the opportunity to witness and we were both blessed.

To me baptism was to die to self, and to rise to new life in Christ. This is just what God did to me through the weeks of hard testing and brokenness. I was struggling to do everything in my own strength, and when I failed I went to God in tears for help, and tried again. This did not work, and I then realized that serving God was not a project but an overflow, produced by waiting on God. So I waited on Him, then I realized that it was not just waiting, but worshipping in spirit and truth, being filled by His Holy Spirit, that produced the overflow.

I then got the victory and found I was no longer affected by the hardness of the work, but was doing it in God's strength.

Waiting on God then becomes continual (praying without ceasing) and the overflow then also becomes continual. As one constantly abides in God's presence, so His Holy Spirit can be released through one's life. No longer is one controlled by the outer man that impacts the inner man with its problems and hurts, but because one has died to the outer man and is constantly given up to the higher God in continual fellowship, the innner man is able to control the outer man and handle life in a more Christ-like manner. Through this one can enter into a new dimension of living for Christ: inwardly living in God's presence, and beginning outwardly, as the Holy Spirit is released, to live a victorious Christian life of full-time service.

After lunch I went for a walk around the ship to explore it and the Lord even taught me more.

Walk down into the belly of this ship,
Everywhere men are hard at work on repairs.
But this ship was originally made perfect,
It is the rust of outside influence that destroys.

So My Spirit is at work in your life
Cleaning up and repairing your body,
For where the rust of sin needs to be scrapped
So the healing ointment of My love repairs

And so My work shall be completed,
And the original product shall be revealed
And as the Anastasias shall sail from port to port
So shall the resurrection of My life flow through you.

And as if He had not taught me enough, He gave me a word of encouragement for those lovely people on board that evening:

You are the people of God, those of which His love flows through.
You have yielded yourselves to God and He has changed the inner self.
His Word is full of power and truth, and this He has given to you.
He wants to express Himself anew, and pour Himself through you.

Break before His presence, that His ointment may pour forth,
Live within His Spirit, that has power to heal and save,
Live to God's great glory, that His face may shine through you
And the Spirit of our God shall be released to many more.

They received this word of encouragement from the Lord and asked me to write it down for them, which I did later. We then went into a time of prayer for the earthquake in Italy. The team wanted to leave by Friday, but still had not got permission to take the Volkswagen into Italy.

The next two days sped by. I had to return to Israel on the Thursday, and the same day the couple were returning. They had had a little boy and already everyone was excited about it and preparing for their return.

I got up early on Thursday to join in the 6.30 am prayer meeting as usual, though they had again been praying all night. Wonderful news: though they still were not allowed to take the Volkswagen into Italy, they were allowed to take in a mini-bus instead. This was much better, as now they could take in much more clothing, blankets and vital necessities, and the team were hard at work getting everything organized.

I said goodbye, and got into the trawler to leave for the mainland. As they were on their way to collect the couple with a new baby in their family, I was given a lift right down to the docks. The timing of everything was again so very perfect.

Chapter 20

Victory in Rhodes

Having gone to sleep outside on deck, I woke up to find myself in a howling wind and prayed for the hurricane to stop. I had come outside to sleep because I did not like all the drunken men and the filth downstairs.

It was quite a shock to one's system to face this, after the sheltered love on the Youth With A Mission ship, and I was still feeling sensitive to all that God was doing in my life. I really needed to stay on the ship longer. Anyway, I sank down deeper into my sleeping bag to try and get some shelter from the wind, but simply got caught up with my thoughts...

'I've seen much, done much, floating from Christian group to Christian group like a loose particle, that settles for a moment, then blows on.

'This is what I have called freedom: different countries, different places, and different experiences. But the Christian body is still the same wherever you go, rooted in the deep love of God.

'It's this deep love which is becoming my security and I realise I must soon again attach myself to part of this large body, which spreads itself throughout the world like an enormous spreading plant, rooting itself deep into the Kingdom of God.

'It's then, as I commit myself to it, that greater growth in my life will occur, causing greater love to spread out from me towards others.

'Man is complex, shaped by many conditions of life and without God he is lost, striving to find himself and satisfying himself with short moments of joy in various avenues of life.

'Man may be confused by sin, but he is still very human and there is beauty in every heart, just seeking its release.

'Only love and understanding can reveal this and only God can release it, for the root of every life is in God who created man.

'Humans are adaptable and though life can be different in such extremes as poverty and wealth, when one is rooted in the love of God, the outward circumstances just die away. A new love emerges which makes the best of every situation, because the inner-self can become so rich in the love of God, that God becomes more precious than any material possession.

'What is freedom? Is it to be physically free to roam the world at your will? Or is it something more?

'To me, I have found that true freedom. Is the release of the Holy Spirit from within you? How can this Spirit be released? When you release your burdens to God. Not just the burdens of sins, or worries, but also of possessing rights, of you yourself surrendering to Him, releasing yourself to Christ. That means dying to self, a breaking of self before the Lord. Then suddenly He releases something through you, for you have come right to the roots of your existence, and just as in your very first cry, so God's love is expressed in new life. His Holy Spirit is released through you to the glory of God.

'So why must we die to self before we can serve God or be free?

'From God's point of view how can He be released though us, when we bind ourselves with ourselves? Fear of rejection – what will they think? – pride – selfishness – self-interests – so many things.

From our point of view how can we be free, if we are still self-conscious, insecure, in bondage to material things, lazy, or closed to God's Word by our own hardness caused by many circumstances?

'But if we yield all this to God, breaking ourselves from their power over us and from the old self that controlled us, then God can replace these things with His new life, and as we then live under His control, so we are set free from ourselves to be ourselves – the original person God created us to be. As we simply rest in God's love and simply **be**, becoming purified from the lost world, so His Spirit is released in us. We are then able to give ourselves to people completely free, and thus allow God's love to flow forth.

'This does not mean we escape from responsibilities or problems, but we are set free to deal to with them victoriously with a clear mind, free from influence and confusion from the old self, and free to hear and obey God.

'This was glorious stuff I was learning and I wanted to achieve it . . .'

The storm was getting worse, but I didn't even care. I simply pulled the sleeping bag over my head, worshipped God and fell asleep.

Next morning the wind had died down. A bit cold, salty and damp, I climbed out of my sleeping bag, still dressed, and hung the sleeping bag up to dry off in the morning sun.

I then decided to go downstairs, but the smell of vomit, beer and cigarettes quickly chased me up on deck again.

Soon I got chatting to a very pleasant English girl and her fiancé. It was then that I discovered why my handbag was so heavy. It was full of Greek tracts that we had been giving out on one of the outreaches from the ship. 'Oh well, I will have to post them back to the ship from Rhodes,' I thought, 'so I'll take them with me when we land.'

We arrived at Rhodes by 10.00 am. As the ship needed some repairs, we were to leave the ship for eight hours, which I did not mind at all, as I had more time to explore. So I set off, together with my newfound friends.

The streets were still wet after last night's storm. We turned off the wide harbour area into the narrow streets of the old city. I waited as my two friends bought some souvenirs at a quaint little shop, and then walking on up the street, heard what sounded like someone preaching.

The filming of 'The Acts of Peter and Paul'

'Shall we see what's going on?' I asked.

'OK with us,' they said, as we followed the sound.

Soon we came to the city square where there were very many people dressed in old-fashioned clothes. We asked someone what was going on.

'Oh, they are filming *The Acts of Peter and Paul,*' came the answer, 'that's the Apostle Paul preaching now.'

'Thank you.'

We got as close as we could so that we could hear. He was a good actor, dynamic and to the point. He was preaching straight out of Scripture and on the things of the Holy Spirit.

Before we knew it, the preaching came to an end and the people began to mill about as there was a break.

'What's this about the Holy Spirit?' my friend asked me.

So I began to tell her. At that one of the actors began to listen too, so I spoke a little louder so that she could hear. She then called her friends over, so that they could also hear, and asked another question about the Holy Spirit. I answered her and still others came.

'Please tell us everything about the Holy Spirit,' they asked me. 'We belong to the Greek Orthodox Church, but we don't get much teaching about the Holy Spirit and now we are part of this film, we want to know everything.'

I was now sharing quite loudly and there were over thirty people around me, some waving hands wanting to ask another question.

'Lord, help me,' I prayed silently, and then went on to tell them how to get baptised in the Holy Spirit. Everyone wanted to get baptised in the Holy Spirit, so I got them to pray the sinner's prayer out loud after me and ask the Lord to give them the Holy Spirit.

The Lord did just that. Some of the people began to cry, others just bowed their heads quietly, but the Lord was working; that was for sure.

I just stood there praying quietly in tongues. I was not sure what to do next, so just waited for the Lord to complete His work with them. Then I remembered the tracts!

I got them out of my handbag ready to give out. These tracts would explain to them in their own language, Greek, what they had just done and would give good advice on how to live the new life baptised in the Holy Spirit.

I then prayed a 'Thank you' prayer with them, for what the Lord had just done for them and offered them the tracts. There was quite a rush for these and not enough to go round, so some of them got out pens and paper and began to copy the tracts. Others came and asked a few more questions and some even gave me their names and addresses, so that I could post them more tracts or books about the Holy Spirit.

I was filled with wonder and awe at what the Lord had just done for these lovely people. There was so much hunger for the Lord and so very few people to help them. 'Why are the ministers of the churches not teaching these vital wonders of

God that equip the people to live a victorious Christian life?' I thought.

I also realised that if I had remembered to give the tracts back, if I had not been there that moment, if my English friends had not asked that vital question at that moment, if I had not been bold enough to speak out loud for the Lord in obedience to Him, these people may not have had the chance of receiving the Holy Spirit into their lives. Even the ship had broken down at the right moment.

In fact the Lord appeared to have arranged everything down to the smallest detail, not only for today, but also for this whole trip.

If I had not missed my boat to Greece, how could I have been picked up to work on the YWAM ship? If I had missed that glorious opportunity, I would also have missed finding out how important it is to obey God straight away and not take three weeks to do it, as I had with the money that God told me to send them.

In fact I had actually lost the control over my own life when I suddenly only had $20 to live on and God had done all the rest. He had taught me so much and had also given me a far better holiday than I ever could have managed on my own, and right now I still had $18 left for the last month in Israel working for the Baptist village. 'I might even be able to buy my mother that long skirt!' I thought.

I also thought, 'if God can use an insignificant shy girl such as me, how much more can He use others?'

He can use mightily anybody who dedicates their life to Him, just as in the days of His disciples and does it not say in Scripture: *'Truly, truly I say to you, he who believes in me, will also do the works that I do, and greater works than these will he do, because I go to the Father, whatever you ask in my name I will do it, that the Father may be glorified in the Son'* (John 14:2).

End? No, this is not the end, it is rather the beginning as we respond to God.

Chapter 21

The Epilogue

Yes, for me, this was just the beginning of many other exciting adventures with the Lord. After returning to Port Elizabeth, I did manage to buy the skirt for my mum. Later I was to meet Wilfrid and get married. The Lord blessed us with much success in the riding school and when the owners decided to sell Longfield, we actually had enough to buy twenty acres of land.

The next adventure came with the building up of a Christian holiday farm and a riding school on this land. We saw many wonderful miracles of provision as in faith we built it up. But that would be a book on its own!

During the following ten years many children and young people came to this holiday farm. Many became Christians, including some through the story of Jacky Boy's miraculous healing. Until one day when he died of old age many children were still learning to ride on Jacky Boy. He was then a good 21 years old. We gave him a Christian burial in his favourite place by the lake where he dropped.

The next phase of our life was our call to England. As we did not want to leave our beloved Spring Valley Holiday Farm and Riding Centre unless the Lord really was calling us, we laid out a fleece before the Lord. To confirm His call to us, we asked the Lord for a job in England within the next twenty-four hours: no phone call, and we would stay where we were. We did not get one phone call from England within twenty-four hours, but two phone calls offering us jobs – a double confirmation.

The move took all the obedience we could muster. It was not easy in England, but it brought us closer to Jesus as a result, and that is worth everything.

After two years working at the two jobs that we had been offered over the phone in South Africa, we managed to save enough money to buy a piece of land in Oxfordshire – also twenty-acres.

Over the next five years the Lord enabled us to build up a fine riding centre with the best facilities, and including two retreat chalets. At present we are building a Christian Centre which will be used for retreats, Christian weekends and for revival and healing meetings.

My beginnings with the Lord, though, were never forgotten, but built on in greater strength. Little did I know that Jacky Boy's story would be as welcome in England. Little did I know that the book I wrote at 'Spring Valley', called *The Biblical Approach to Basic Horsemanship'*, would be sold worldwide, and that I would get invited to different countries to train riding instructors to teach the Biblical Approach to Horsemanship to others. Little did I know that Jacky Boy and the Biblical Approach to Horsemanship would even be shown on British television. I was even to set up an organisation called 'Christians in Horsemanship', under the umbrella of Christians in Sport.

The obedience I learnt on the Greek ship was to become more developed as I grew in the knowledge and presence of God.

As I was able to come into God's presence, the Lord would pour out His love, peace and joy on me in such a way that obedience then became a joy rather than a sacrifice.

Paying our own airfare to go and work hard in another country for a week or so became a pleasure; and exceedingly worthwhile. We saw God at work in His glorious and beautiful ways. There is nothing on this earth that can compare with the pleasure and joy of serving our wonderful Lord and Saviour. There is no better life than the yielding of ourselves to be changed by Him, commissioned by Him, and used by Him. There is no better way than walking in total and complete obedience, for even though it may appear to be a sacrifice at first, it results in the highest of blessings; not only to others but to us as well. For the truth is, *'It is more blessed to give than to receive.'* One of these trips was to the Fire Over Kenya Conference in November and December 2001.

Fire Over Kenya Conference

Ruth and I, along with the Bishop, left the tar roads, then we left the gravel roads, then we left the tracks. We were driving down river beds and across the most rugged terrain, past mud kraals. We were the first whites to come here in three years.

We stopped to join in a funeral. Already the needs of the people were getting to us, six deaths a day in this area alone, 700 a day nationally. This was beyond wild, it's raw and desperate.

We eventually arrived at the Bishop's house – a mud kraal, bamboo bathroom and mud privy.

The people only live for today for tomorrow is not certain. Ruth and I were up early and interceded together. We cried out to the Lord like never before. We could not stop crying for the needs and that the Lord would heal them. 'If I cry with compassion through your eyes like this, so too shall I also heal them through your hands like this,' blurted out of me from the Lord.

We went back to the kraal for breakfast. A boy possessed by evil spirits was brought to us by his mother; he could not stand, he was falling all over the place convulsing. We felt so inadequate to help him, but prayed anyway. To our amazement, as we cast the demons out, the boy became normal and walked home.

We then went to the orphanage. I spoke on the story of Dion the orphan and how he discovered the Father's love. Ruth and I then prayed the Father's love on each and every one and they all received from the Lord. We also prayed for healing for heads, stomachs, a leaking ear and TB and the Lord healed them all.

The chief came to see us, which is an honour and he welcomed us personally. We then prayed for the beginning of the conference that was to start at 8.00 pm. 'Rest in Me, don't strive for I will do it,' said the Lord.

We then had supper. The Bishop had brought home a visitor – an army general who shared supper with us. He was nothing to do with the conference but wanted to become a Christian so we prayed for him. He then told us about his very sick wife dying of TB. She could not stand up, could hardly speak. She just slept all the time. Again we felt so helpless but we prayed for her, laying hands on him as proxy. The man then walked home. To his amazement, he saw his wife come towards him. She had suddenly been 100% healed at the time of the prayer. She was so happy. Oh the joy.

After supper we walked to the meeting in the moonlight and also joined others on the way to the conference. I gave the gospel and healing message and asked those who needed healing to come forward. About 30 rushed forward and they all got healed and at least six testified. The first healings were four people with blind or bad eyes instantly healed, a lady and child with malaria instantly healed, four babies with fever, one hepatitis, four people with stomach pain, etc. Another instant healing was a man who had a damaged head from a fall that caused his left arm to be lame. Now he could move his arm normally. We also prayed for deliverances and proxy for the very sick at home including a husband with dysentery. We then thanked and praised the Lord in song. The joy and the praise was ecstatic for this was Jesus doing it.

It was Thursday the 29th November. In the morning we went to Homa Bay, which means 'Sickness Bay'. I spoke at 3.00 pm and 8.00 pm. During the day we prayed for 25 people and some testified of the healings. I spoke on the fruits of the Holy Spirit and Rivers of Living Water. The healings were similar to Wednesday night, plus more eye problems that were also instantly healed.

Friday 30th, 10.00 am: I gave a talk to the pastors on the gifts of the Holy Spirit. I then prayed for the impartation of the gifts of healing and deliverance on them. The Holy Spirit came down powerfully as I prayed for them. Most of the pastors began to shake and cry under the power of the Holy Spirit. We prayed for 42 people that day and 11 gave testimonies, some wonderful ones, especially the sick at home that had been healed of sickness and disease, including a very sick child now able to come to the meeting too.

Saturday, 1st December: Ruth spoke on the Father's love, then I spoke but felt the Lord leading me to get them to pray quietly. This I did and the Lord gave me a prophecy in response to a tongue a lady gave. All of a sudden the Holy Spirit of God came down on the meeting like a wind; everyone began to cry and pray out. Suddenly people ran to the front, fell down on their knees and cried out to God. Some people tending their cattle in the distance, left the cattle and ran to the tent, into the tent and up to the front where they fell down on their knees in repentance to become Christians.

The Holy Spirit was so strong. I did not know what to do. I did not feel it right to lay hands on them just then, for God was doing the work. So many different things at the same time. People were shaking, crying, wailing, praying out loud in tongues. People were being delivered, healed in their seats, filled with God's love and set free. I never saw anything like this, so beautiful was His presence. After 15 minutes or so it quietened down and Ruth and I prayed for three people all instantly healed, and twelve had been healed in their seats. It was a glorious time with God.

I then asked the pastors to come forward and anointed them with oil and commissioned them to go out in Jesus' name. Some of them were powerfully touched, especially their wives. One lady from Tanzania, Esther, was totally slain in the Holy Spirit and great anointing. Fifty people were healed that day and 21 gave testimonies. The pastors who had received the gift of healing were praying with us and everyone got healed regardless of who was praying for them. That night I heard the witch-doctors on their drums and prayed against any curses they may pour on us.

Sunday, 2nd December: The fire of God came down again. I spoke on the temple of the Holy Spirit. I then got the people to pray and open their hearts for God to come in and He did. The Holy Spirit came down and it got noisy again. People came forward to accept Jesus into their hearts, others to be baptised in the Holy Spirit, others for deliverances and healings. We were then about to close the service, ten more people came forward, and the Holy Spirit came down yet again. Eyes were being instantly healed, the swollen side of a man (from a wound) came down in size in front of our eyes, now suddenly he could lift his arm up, which he could not do before. A sore neck and throat healed so the lady could move her neck which she could not do before without pain, stomachs, heads, etc. Fifty-three healed in this last service and 26 testified of instant healings. Plus one from a confused mind yesterday now healed. A child's eyes healed yesterday now perfectly clear, another lady who had painful eyes for two years and very blurred vision had been instantly healed. Ruth prayed for 10 from the 'Homa Bay Healing and Happiness team' and they were very deeply touched by God. Bishop Dominic then closed the meeting. Altogether we had prayed for 200 people. Only God can do this.

Monday, 3rd December: We were able to visit the wife the Lord had miraculously healed of TB. She was excited to meet us and to show us how well the Lord had healed her. We went into their home and prayed and thanked the Lord with them and felt the beautiful presence of the Lord. We then went through Homa Bay. A cripple asked me for some food so I gave him a biscuit and prayed for him. He was paralysed from the waist down having contracted polio as a child. He could only move his legs with his hands. After the prayer he could wriggle his toes and move his legs on their own with no hands. Then I was asked to pray for a blind man and he was instantly healed. Ruth gave a short gospel message and led twenty children and four adults to the Lord. She prayed for a man who'd had painful feet for two years and he was instantly healed.

That night I was kept awake by the witch-doctors' drumming all night, so prayed against their curses again. I told Bishop Dominic about it and he said it was true. They were very angry about the healings as it meant lost income for them.

Tuesday, 4th December: Drove to Kisumu. It was lunch time, the fourth day without food. I asked the Lord if I should eat. 'Eat, My child, for I am doing it and will continue to do it.' I also managed to take the most welcome shower of my life. We then took Ruth to the airport as she needed to return home and then continued our journey. We crossed the Equator and confirmed a meeting in the jungle where millions of fireflies flew and booked into a hotel.

Wednesday, 5th December: 5.30 am – the witch-doctors at last have stopped chanting and drumming, very unusual in the middle of the week. It worried me how effective the bush telegraph is and felt they were following our movements, but the Lord said, 'Walk forth My child, for no evil shall touch you. Rest in Me, My child, for it is I that shall do it through you. Just walk in oneness with Me.' After this word I felt that even an army of witch-doctors could not deter us.

The first church we visited was Uhangja church near Lake Victoria – 45 came. All got baptised in the Holy Spirit, three gave their lives to the Lord and eleven were healed. Chest, ears, malaria, backaches, asthma and confused minds. We also prayed for the leaders.

The second church was Kanji church. We drove into the jungle as far as we could then walked. It was a new church made of sticks and mats. I preached the gospel – one new convert responded, three baptised in the Holy Spirit, twelve healings, three deliverances. The first the Lord set free was a boy set free from epilepsy very powerfully. Other healings were headaches, backaches, stomach, arthritis of joints, malaria, and children were healed.

The third church was being built. We prayed for six people – a dog bite, stomachs, family problems, a deliverance and anointing of the leader for gifts of healing and deliverance.

The fourth church was Kasuma church. We spoke to elders and pastors on the temple of God and how to reach Him in prayer, how to keep our temples clean and receive Him into us, then prayed God's anointing on each one.

Thursday, 6th December: We left for Massai land over beautiful forested hills and tea farms, visited one and spoke to all the children, sang and prayed with them.

Friday, 7th December: We left at 7.00 am and arrived at Massai land at 9.00 am. We found a boy called Nicodemus who took us to a naming ceremony, showed us the Massai home, very dark, a fire in middle and tiny bedrooms coming off it. Then they showed us their goats and camels. We watched the blessing of the woman, then the chief came and I spoke on animal care and medicines. We then prayed with them and left for Nairobi.

Saturday, 8th December: The meeting was cancelled because of unrest, ten killed over rent problems. So we met Pastor Daniel and prayed for a missionary in bondage and Lord set her free.

Sunday, 9th December: We spoke at a small tin-shack church in the poorest of poor areas. Two were baptised in the Holy Spirit, two were instantly healed, a neck and stomach, and one other problem solved by the Lord. We then went for lunch on the way to the airport. A lady was in acute pain in her stomach. We prayed and the Lord removed the pain and she ate with us.

This trip changed our lives, for the words of our feeble prayers were enough for His miracles, His healings. To live close to Jesus does change you. All hardness goes, you melt before His presence into His compassion and love for His people. I was overwhelmed at God's great love for His people. After the conference many left the witch-doctors and became Christians as many more testified of the healings of Jesus, including two medically proven healings of HIV AIDS.

Serving God is not a project, but an overflow, produced by waiting on God, and being filled with His love, His joy, His peace, and His compassion for others. When we wait on God in this way, and I always look forward to it everyday, it becomes the joy of our lives to have this glorious fellowship with God. Then the overflow is always that of joy and expectancy. The Lord always has surprises in store for us, as He flows His love, deliverance and healing power through your hands onto the person you pray for. Sometimes it is as though your hands turn into a tap of God's power. You will see people instantly healed or set free, filled with the incredible joy of the Lord. The Lord is able to do these things, even through the weak feeble hands of a mere human being.

The Lord is glorious; He is wonderful; He is all-loving and He loves you.

If you would like to respond to the Lord, and I am sure you would, maybe for the first time, maybe as a re-commitment, or maybe desiring baptism in the Holy Spirit, say one of the following prayers, as appropriate, now...

First time or re-commitment:

Dear Lord Jesus, I come to You as I am,
Please forgive me, Lord, when I have sinned in thought,
In word, in deed, in things left undone.
Please come into my life as my Lord and Saviour.

For baptism in the Holy Spirit:

Please baptise me in your glorious Holy Spirit,
Thank you Lord. Amen.

Now you will be able to pray daily, read your Bible with a new understanding, and join a church or Christian fellowship of your choice. Live out your new Christian life day by day, allowing the Lord to guide you and help you live it. Tell someone about your new commitment to the Lord. Make some new Christian friends, for we all need one another.

If you should require further prayer or healing, write to me or phone me at the address on page 160.

> 'May God bless you, may His hand be upon your life, and may He strengthen you and fill you with His perfect, love, joy and peace. Amen.'

The Standlake Equestrian Centre and Ranch

The Standlake Equestrian Centre and Ranch is an inter-denominational riding school, residential ranch and outreach centre, devoted to encouraging people in the Lord and to spreading the Gospel in any way possible.

People can come and stay in ranch-style accommodation, have ministry for healing and wholeness, learn to ride horses, go on forest walks, boat on the lake, and relax and enjoy the beauty surrounding them.

For more information, or for the ordering of books, write to:

Suzanne Pillans
Standlake Equestrian Centre and Ranch
Downs Road
Standlake
Witney
Oxon OX29 7UH

Tel: 01865 300099
email (wpillans@aol.com)